"There are a number of good books available on reconciling science and Christian theology, particularly creation and evolution. The value of such books to various audiences depends, of course, on some shared assumptions. Carlson and Longman's book is especially important for anyone who perceives conflict between evolutionary theory and Scripture. While sharing a commitment to scriptural infallibility and a generally literalist reading, they nonetheless show that none of the multiple creation stories in the Old Testament precludes the acceptance of contemporary science. I recommend it highly."

Nancey Murphy, professor of Christian philosophy,
Fuller Theological Seminary

"Carlson and Longman argue clearly and patiently for a truce in the war between science and Christianity. When taken together, they give a more complete picture of the human drama, and they can be brought together if we learn to respect the unique perspectives they each bring to the conversation. The authors guide readers to important principles of biblical interpretation, the nature of scientific and theological knowledge, and most importantly a faithful and contextual reading of the all-important creation stories of Genesis. This book is an excellent and irenic introduction to a timely topic where cool heads and broad learning are greatly needed."

Peter Enns, senior fellow, biblical studies, The BioLogos Foundation

"Readers struggling with evolution will find this discussion by Carlson and Longman most helpful. The authors combine a robust respect for science in all its manifestations with a high view of Scripture. The result is a solid argument that there need be no conflict between the biblical and scientific accounts of our origins."

Karl Giberson, author of *Saving Darwin: How to Be a Christian and Believe in Evolution*, and senior fellow, The BioLogos Foundation

SCIENCE, CREATION

AND THE

BIBLE

RECONCILING RIVAL THEORIES OF ORIGINS

Richard F. Carlson and Tremper Longman III

IVP Academic
An imprint of InterVarsity Press
Downers Grove, Illinois

InterVarsity Press
P.O. Box 1400, Downers Grove, IL 60515-1426
World Wide Web: www.ivpress.com
E-mail: email@ivpress.com

InterVarsity Press® is the book-publishing division of InterVarsity Christian Fellowship/USA®, a
movement of students and faculty active on campus at hundreds of universities, colleges and schools
of nursing in the United States of America, and a member movement of the International Fellowship
of Evangelical Students. For information about local and regional activities, write Public Relations
Dept., InterVarsity Christian Fellowship/USA, 6400 Schroeder Rd., P.O. Box 7895, Madison, WI
53707-7895, or visit the IVCF website at <www.intervarsity.org>.

Unless otherwise indicated, all Scripture quotations are taken from the Holy Bible, New Living
Translation, copyright ©1996, 2004. Used by permission of Tyndale House Publishers, Inc.,
Wheaton, Illinois 60189. All rights reserved.

Design: Cindy Kiple
Images: outer space explosion: pederk/iStockphoto
     stone tablet: The Flood Tablet. Neo-Assyrian. From the palace library of King Ashurbanipal,
     Nineveh, northern Iraq at British Museum, London, Great Britain. ©The Trustees of the
     British Museum/Art Resource, NY

ISBN 978-0-8308-3889-9

Printed in the United States of America ∞

Library of Congress Cataloging-in-Publication Data

Carlson, Richard F., 1936-
  Science, creation, and the Bible: reconciling rival theories of
origins / Richard F. Carlson, Tremper Longman III.
     p. cm.
  Includes bibliographical references and index.
  ISBN 978-0-8308-3889-9 (pbk.: alk. paper)
  1. Creationism. 2. Creation. 3. Religion and science. 4. Bible.
  O.T. Genesis I-II—Criticism, interpretation, etc. I. Longman,
Tremper. II. Title.
  BS651.C333 2010
  231.7'652—dc22
                                 2010019871

| P | 18 | 17 | 16 | 15 | 14 | 13 | 12 | 11 | 10 | 9 | 8 | 7 | 6 | 5 | 4 | 3 | 2 | 1 |
| Y | 25 | 24 | 23 | 22 | 21 | 20 | 19 | 18 | 17 | 16 | 15 | 14 | 13 | 12 | 11 | 10 |

Before the mountains were born,

before you gave birth to the earth and the world,

from beginning to end,

you are God.

PSALM 90:2

Contents

Acknowledgments

THE AUTHORS ARE GRATEFUL TO Jason Hine for his contribution to the early writing of this book when it was taking form. He also aided in the development of the themes and content as he contributed to and took part in presentations at church seminars where the ideas for the book were initially tried on live audiences. Many people have helped in forming this book through their commentary at seminars, Bible study classes, Sunday school classes, and college and seminary courses. Jason was a participant in many of these.

Dr. Rebecca Rio-Jellife played a crucial role as adviser while the book was being written. Her helpful critical comments aided in the formation of the logic of the presentation, and she provided valuable tutoring regarding style during the writing. We thank her for her extraordinary efforts and the time she devoted to the preparation of the manuscript. She had a hand in all that is good about this book.

Introduction

MANY CHRISTIANS ARE TORN BETWEEN their belief in the creation narrative in the Bible and the conclusions of contemporary science, views that seem irreconcilable. Conflict exists over a number of issues. This book has grown out of our belief in the possibility of reconciling modern science with our Christian faith. One can commit oneself to the Christian faith but also perceive our world through the lens of science. Science and faith together may give a more complete understanding of our universe and our world, including ourselves.

This book began to take shape many years ago, long before the coauthors met. Fifty years ago Richard Carlson began to study physics; at the same time he was drawn into Christianity through a Christian group on the campus of the University of Redlands. Both pursuits gave direction for ensuing years. Physics became a passion that led to graduate school at the University of Minnesota, followed by teaching at the University of Redlands, and years of nuclear physics research. However, his growing Christian faith became the foundation for all of his life. He became aware of a deep conflict between the biblical understanding of creation and the contemporary scientific picture on beginnings. This troubled him because it seemed that these unlike enterprises addressed the same phenomenon, God's creation in two books, the Bible and science. The resolution of this con-

flict has been on Richard's mind ever since. To that end, he took a
course of study at Fuller Theological Seminary toward a master's de-
gree in theology and biblical studies. Now he could examine the conflict. After years of studying both sides of the issue, he has concluded
that the "irreconcilable" viewpoints are different but complementary
readings of creation accounts.

Coauthor Tremper Longman III has no scientific heritage. As a
non-Christian, he learned about evolution in high school and simply
looked with skepticism at the biblical creation account. Before he entered college at Ohio Wesleyan, he became a Christian, and in the
next years he met with friends in study to nurture their growing
faith. His studies continued at Westminster Theological Seminary,
where he became committed to the exploration of Scripture. Doctoral
study at Yale in Near Eastern languages and literature prepared him
for teaching and thinking about the Bible, particularly about the
creation-evolution problem. He taught at Westminster Seminary for
eighteen years and the past eleven years has taught at Westmont College as the Robert Gundry Professor of Biblical Studies. Over these
years Tremper has taught and written a book on Genesis. He has seen
many students enter his classes having established their own understanding of the Genesis account of creation, which they consider to
be correct. Some turn their view into a matter of orthodoxy, insisting
that interpreting Genesis 1 as other than twenty-four-hour creation
days is to cave in to "secular science" and to depart from God's truth.
Tremper has considered the creation-evolution issue in light of his
studies of biblical teaching about creation, and he also finds the conflict to be satisfactorily resolvable.

Recently our paths crossed for the first time, and we decided to
collaborate on a joint study of the creation-evolution conflict using
both theological and scientific approaches. Our aim is to bring the
two enterprises together at a valid and peacemaking position, fully
satisfactory to Christians.

The conflict arose when Charles Darwin, in his 1859 work, *The Origin of Species,* concluded that his exploration and observations implied

that the creation of the earth and life on the earth differed from the six-day Genesis 1 creation account. Darwin's scientific conclusions undermined the belief of many Christians that the biblical account accurately portrayed historical and scientific understandings of beginnings. But the seeds of the conflict were planted earlier in the nineteenth century when progress on the study of the earth produced evidence suggesting that the earth may be older than the six creation days of Genesis and that life progressed from earlier forms. During the past two hundred years, all of science, including earth science, biology, cosmology and physics, have advanced. The developments in technology in the late nineteenth and early twentieth centuries opened the door to the microworld of the molecule, atom, nucleus and fundamental particle, and into the relativistic world of extremely high speeds. Continuing research in science and developments in technology provide us today with a more complete understanding of the earth, the cosmos and all life forms. It is not surprising therefore that the Genesis 1 creation narrative, unchanged over the years since it was formulated by its sacred author some three thousand to four thousand years ago, differs significantly from current scientific views.

Prior to the advances in science over the past 200 years, there was no scientific or historical challenge to the literal reading of Genesis creation. And earlier theories on how language works also supported a literal reading. But the controversy in the past 150 years over the understanding of Genesis and the reliability of contemporary science has led us to try to resolve this conflict while affirming our Christian faith and scientific conclusions.

We profess our deep commitment to Christian faith and the biblical teaching about creation. At the same time, we believe contemporary science addresses questions on *how* physical and biological processes began and continue to develop, while theology and philosophy answer *why* for the same questions. The creation-evolution conflict hinges on two issues: (1) the question of the trustworthiness of contemporary scientific understanding of the beginnings of the universe, the earth and life on the earth, and (2) the question of the faithful reading of the two creation passages in Genesis 1:1–2:3 and Genesis 2:4-25 in their literal or nonliteral forms.

Why would such a long-standing conflict concern us? First, our purpose is to encourage all Christians to ground their theological and scientific beliefs in an impartial search for truth. Second, we want to remove false barriers that discourage non-Christians from considering the Christian gospel. We want to attempt to present an accurate description of both the scientific and the theological enterprises, including suggestions for a systematic reading of the Bible. Above all, we hope to suggest a way to resolve the creation-evolution conflict and bring conciliation between scientific and spiritual truths that underlie faith. To that end we propose the following thesis:

The first two chapters of Genesis, which accurately present two accounts of creation in terms of ancient Hebrew scientific observations and their historical understanding, are neither historical nor scientific in the twenty-first-century literal sense. Instead, the underlying message of these chapters applies for all time and constitutes a complete statement of the worldview of the Hebrew people in the ancient Near East. They accurately understood the universe in terms of why God created it but not how in the modern scientific and historical sense. This worldview, markedly different from those of their pagan neighbors, articulates the principles underlying their understanding of the relation of God to the universe, their relation to the true God, and their relation to each other and to the created order.

If the first two chapters of Genesis present the fundamental character of the ancient Hebrew people rather than a factual scientific account of beginnings that meets contemporary standards, then it is not appropriate to try to reconcile contemporary science with the Genesis accounts.

The science-faith conflict arises from the two sets of sources (chapter one), the theological and the contemporary scientific. First, the theological information in the creation account of Genesis 1 constitutes what most Christians regard as *the* Genesis creation material, including the scientific and historical data as understood by the ancient sacred writer. But Genesis presents more about creation than simply Genesis 1, for Genesis 2 constitutes a second creation account, one that has similarities to but also differences from the first. Genesis 1 gives a cosmological view of creation, whereas Genesis 2 focuses on the creation of and provisions for humanity. The second source of information, the scientific data, depicts the beginning and development of the universe, the earth and life on the earth, including humanity. American Christians differ in their interpretation of the biblical material and their evaluation of the legitimacy of modern science. But they agree that the Bible is the foundational source that provides the basis for all Christian knowledge and application. This application includes the four American views on creation and science. These viewpoints are principally a consequence of differences in interpreting the Bible and lead to differences in the understanding of the Genesis 1 creation narrative. In addition, the four viewpoints represent different evaluations of contemporary science. Herein lies a good part of the source of the conflict.

Identifying the characteristics of each field, theology and science, may contribute toward resolving the creation-evolution conflict. The interests, methods, sources of information, limitations, their relationship to common sense, the need for careful interpretation of basic data and how each can contribute to the other are noted (chapter two).

Theology and science are each seekers after truth. The primary source for theology is the Bible, and we endorse the high view of the Bible as articulated by the 1978 Chicago Statement on Biblical Inerrancy. In science, measurable data along with the hypothetical-deductive method produce its results. Each enterprise has aspects that are counterintuitive. In Christian theology, Jesus is understood as both fully God and fully human. Science shows that all entities in the universe exhibit themselves sometimes as particles and sometimes as waves. Fast objects shrink and get heavier. Inability to understand a phenomenon or a concept is not necessarily a criterion of its truthfulness.

A systematic interpretation of controversial biblical passages constitutes a crucial step in understanding their application today, especially to resolve the theology-science conflict (chapter three). The differences among Christians in their understanding of the Bible (in particular, Genesis) are a major source of contention in the conflict. Among the many helpful biblical interpretive methods, our chapter three focuses on one that carefully considers content, context and the intent of the biblical writer. In addition, special emphasis is given to the nonliteral genre of parable or story, first noting Jesus' extensive and effective use of parable and then examining the use of story and parable in the writing of trusted Christian authors. Jesus shows that parable and story are effective and legitimate genres. The identification of the genre of a biblical passage can be difficult but important, including in the cases of Genesis 1 and 2.

Next is a discussion of the Bible as possessing both divine and human (incarnational) aspects. The incarnational can be observed in a biblical author writing with the culture, context and experience of the first recipients of the passage or book in mind. This ensures for those recipients an accurate understanding of the message. Hence, couching the Genesis creation accounts using the form of other ancient Near Eastern accounts, familiar to the Hebrews, is not surprising and is legitimate. A parallel exists here between Jesus and the Bible, as both are divine and incarnational. The incarnational aspect of each demonstrates God's accommodation to real humans at specific times and places. The chapter ends with a short discussion of the interpretation of scientific data.

The application of the principle of using Scripture to interpret Scripture constitutes another step in the attempt to understand the message of creation in Genesis through the examination of all principal biblical passages related to creation. From the Old Testament (chapter four), Isaiah 40, Job 38–41, and a bit from the proverbs and the creation psalms are analyzed along with parts of John 1, Colossians 1, Hebrews 1, and Romans 1 and 8 from the New Testament (chapter five). The interpretive method of chapter three is applied, the purpose being to end up with a thorough analysis of the Genesis creation passages (chapter six), all contributing to the attempt to understand the intent for their first ancient hearers/readers. The analyses of the passages in chapters four and five show how the content of the creation story of Genesis 1 and 2 moves throughout the Bible in telling a greater story than simply an ancient scientific and historical account.

Genesis 1 and 2 are correctly understood in terms of accounts of the ancient Hebrew understanding of science and history, but not correctly in modern terms (chapter seven). Instead, Genesis 1 and 2 together contain a second message hidden under the creation story, its importance expected to be consistent with that of other uses of creation throughout the Bible. Our proposal is that the "story under the story" in Genesis 1 and 2 represents the ancient Hebrew's worldview and thus constitutes the primary relevance of these opening chapters in the Bible for all time and for all peoples. These worldview themes are found throughout all of Scripture, implying their relevance for all times, in particular for today. Understanding Genesis 1 and 2 in this way removes the requirement that they be consistent with contemporary science, for they had in the past and now have a much more important role to play.

The current scientific picture of beginnings and subsequent developments of the universe, the earth and life are most likely more valid than invalid. But these "how" explanations cannot be extrapolated to comments on issues beyond those of science. For example, one illegitimate application of cosmology and biological evolutionary theory includes the idea that the understanding of beginnings in terms of naturalistic science implies the nonexistence of God, or that humanity is only a more developed ape. Christians correctly judge these as invalid and dangerous applications, and conclude that science can only legitimately apply to the *how* questions of science.

The plan of this book is to systematically move step by step toward resolution of the conflict. The first step is to note the basic sources of information that lead to the conflict—the biblical information of Genesis 1 and 2 and the scientific understanding of beginnings.

---

①

Theological and Scientific Sources
and Their Interpretation

THE ANALYSIS OF THE CREATION-EVOLUTION conflict begins by taking note of its origin, the information contained in the theological and scientific sources relevant to the problem. These and their conflicting interpretations constitute fundamental factors resulting in the conflict.

THEOLOGICAL SOURCES
The word *genesis* means origin. Most people regard Genesis 1 as the Bible's account of creation. But a second creation account immediately follows in Genesis 2. A complete biblical understanding of creation requires awareness of all biblical writings about creation, analysis of which will be completed in due course.

The biblical translation used throughout this book is the New Living Translation of the Bible. This particular translation was chosen because of our confidence that the scholars who took part in translating and editing this version of the biblical text fulfill their purpose as stated in "A Note to Readers":

> The goal of any Bible translation is to convey the meaning and content of the ancient Hebrew, Aramaic, and Greek texts as ac-

curately as possible to contemporary readers. . . . The resulting translation is easy to read and understand, while also accurately communicating the meaning and content of the original biblical texts.[1]

Genesis 1.

[1]In the beginning God created the heavens and the earth. [2]The earth was formless and empty, and darkness covered the deep waters. And the Spirit of God was hovering over the surface of the waters.

[3]Then God said, "Let there be light," and there was light. [4]And God saw that the light was good. Then he separated the light from the darkness. [5]God called the light "day" and the darkness "night."

And evening passed and morning came, marking the first day.

[6]Then God said, "Let there be a space between the waters, to separate the waters of the heavens from the waters of the earth." [7]And that is what happened. God made this space to separate the waters of the earth from the waters of the heavens. [8]God called the space "sky."

And evening passed and morning came, marking the second day.

[9]Then God said, "Let the waters beneath the sky flow together into one place, so dry ground may appear." And that is what happened. [10]God called the dry ground "land" and the waters "seas." And God saw that it was good. [11]Then God said, "Let the land sprout with vegetation—every sort of seed-bearing plant, and trees that grow seed-bearing fruit. These seeds will then produce the kinds of plants and trees from which they came." And that is what happened. [12]The land produced vegetation—all sorts of seed-bearing plants, and trees with seed-

---

[1]"A Note to Readers," in *Holy Bible—New Living Translation,* 2nd ed. (Wheaton, Ill.: Tyndale House, 2004), p. A65.

bearing fruit. Their seeds produced plants and trees of the same kind. And God saw that it was good. [13]And evening passed and morning came, marking the third day. [14]Then God said, "Let great lights appear in the sky to separate the day from the night. Let them mark off the seasons, days, and years. [15]Let these lights in the sky shine down on the earth." And that is what happened. [16]God made two great lights, the sun and the moon—the larger one to govern the day, and the smaller one to govern the night. He also made the stars. [17]God set these lights in the sky to light the earth, [18]to govern the day and night, and to separate the light from the darkness. And God saw that it was good. [19]And evening passed and morning came, marking the fourth day.

[20]Then God said, "Let the waters swarm with fish and other life. Let the skies be filled with birds of every kind." [21]So God created great sea creatures and every living thing that scurries and swarms in the water, and every sort of bird—each producing offspring of the same kind. And God saw that it was good. [22]Then God blessed them, saying, "Be fruitful and multiply. Let the fish fill the seas, and let the birds multiply on the earth."

[23]And evening passed and morning came, marking the fifth day.

[24]Then God said, "Let the earth produce every sort of animal, each producing offspring of the same kind—livestock, small animals that scurry along the ground, and wild animals." And that is what happened. [25]God made all sorts of wild animals, livestock, and small animals, each able to produce offspring of the same kind. And God saw that it was good.

[26]Then God said, "Let us make human beings in our image, to be like ourselves. They will reign over the fish in the sea, the birds in the sky, the livestock, all the wild animals on the earth,

and the small animals that scurry along the ground."

27So God created human beings in his own image.
In the image of God he created them;
male and female he created them.

28Then God blessed them and said, "Be fruitful and multiply. Fill the earth and govern it. Reign over the fish in the sea, the birds in the sky, and all the animals that scurry along the ground." 29Then God said, "Look! I have given you every seed-bearing plant throughout the earth and all the fruit trees for your food. 30And I have given every green plant as food for all the wild animals, the birds in the sky, and the small animals that scurry along the ground—everything that has life." And that is what happened.

31Then God looked over all he had made, and he saw that it was very good!

And evening passed and morning came, marking the sixth day.

Genesis 2.

1So the creation of the heavens and the earth and everything in them was completed. 2On the seventh day God had finished his work of creation, so he rested from all his work. 3And God blessed the seventh day and declared it holy, because it was the day when he rested from all his work of creation.

4This is the account of the creation of the heavens and the earth.

When the LORD God made the earth and the heavens, 5neither wild plants nor grains were growing on the earth. The LORD God had not yet sent rain to water the earth, and there were no people to cultivate the soil. 6Instead, springs came up from the ground and watered all the land. 7Then the LORD God formed the man from the dust of the ground. He breathed the breath of life into the man's nostrils, and the man became a living person.

8Then the LORD God planted a garden in Eden in the east,

and there he placed the man he had made. [9]The LORD God made all sorts of trees grow up from the ground—trees that were beautiful and that produced delicious fruit. In the middle of the garden he placed the tree of life and the tree of the knowledge of good and evil. [10]A river watered the garden and then flowed out of Eden and divided into four branches. [11]The first branch, called the Pishon, flowed around the entire land of Havilah, where gold is found. [12]The gold of that land is exceptionally pure; aromatic resin and onyx stone are also found there. [13]The second branch, called the Gihon, flowed around the entire land of Cush. [14]The third branch, called the Tigris, flowed east of the land of Asshur. The fourth branch is called the Euphrates.

[15]The LORD God placed the man in the Garden of Eden to tend and watch over it. [16]But the LORD God warned him, "You may freely eat the fruit of every tree in the garden—[17]except the tree of the knowledge of good and evil. If you eat its fruit, you are sure to die."

[18]Then the LORD God said, "It is not good for the man to be alone. I will make a helper who is just right for him." [19]So the LORD God formed from the ground all the wild animals and all the birds of the sky. He brought them to the man to see what he would call them, and the man chose a name for each one. [20]He gave names to all the livestock, all the birds of the sky, and all the wild animals. But still there was no helper just right for him.

[21]So the LORD God caused the man to fall into a deep sleep. While the man slept, the LORD God took out one of the man's ribs and closed up the opening. [22]Then the LORD God made a woman from the rib, and he brought her to the man.

[23]"At last!" the man exclaimed.

"This one is bone from my bone
and flesh from my flesh!
She will be called 'woman,'
because she was taken from 'man.'"

²⁴This explains why a man leaves his father and mother and is joined to his wife, and the two are united into one.

²⁵Now the man and his wife were both naked, but they felt no shame.

INTERPRETATION OF THEOLOGICAL SOURCES

The familiar creation account sometimes referred to as the "Genesis 1 account" continues through Genesis 2:3. But Genesis 2:4-25 constitutes a second creation account, much to the surprise of many Christians.

The reader of a particular translation of the Bible depends on the accuracy of its translators. A higher level source may be found in the Hebrew version of the Old Testament, known as *Biblia Hebraica Stuttgartensia,* and a contemporary version of the Greek New Testament such as the Nestle-Aland version. But most Christians do not read Hebrew or Greek and hence must depend on the quality of the chosen translation. Most modern English translations, including the New International Version, Today's New International Version, the Revised Standard Version, the New Revised Standard Version, the English Standard Version and the New Living Translation all prove satisfactory for biblical passages regarding creation. The Genesis 1 and 2 texts just presented accurately represent the Hebrew and will serve well for the purposes of examining Genesis as a step in addressing the conflict.

Next we turn to a summary of four American viewpoints on the creation-evolution conflict.² Each point of view—creationism, intelligent design, partnership and independence—is associated with a distinct principle of biblical interpretation and evaluation of the relevant science. This provides background important to the resolution of the conflict.

Creationism arose after Darwin published his work that led to the development of the theory of evolution in the mid-nineteenth cen-

---

²Richard F. Carlson, ed., *Science and Christianity: Four Views* (Downers Grove, Ill.: InterVarsity Press, 2000).

tury. Many Christians have found his position to be a threat to the creation account in Genesis 1. These Christians understand the Bible to declare creation as occurring in six days with all entities created in their final form, and certainly not over long spans of time as Darwin concluded. Furthermore, they object to the idea that there was a common ancestor for all living beings, with the human family having emerged only at the end of a long and continuous development of life forms. Young-earth creationists read Genesis 1 in a literal way and conclude that the entire Bible must be so read except in the clear cases of parables. Creationists regard the Genesis 1 creation account to be historically and scientifically accurate in terms of modern knowledge. Advocates have sought to have creationism taught in public-school science classrooms but were dealt a severe blow by the Supreme Court's 1987 *Aguillard v. Louisiana* decision declaring creationism to be a religious movement, and hence forbidden constitutionally for public-school science instruction.

Old-earth creationism is a related movement that interprets the six days of Genesis 1 as implying much longer periods of time in line with cosmologists and earth scientists. They join the young-earth creationists in denying the conclusions of evolutionary biological science. Conflict exists between biological science and all forms of creationism, and between young-earth creationism and physics, cosmology and earth science.

Intelligent design (ID) grew out of creationism after the Supreme Court's *Aguillard* decision. Sympathetic with the anti-evolutionary stance of creationism, ID has attempted to avoid the appearance of the religious aspect of creationism that led to the Supreme Court's decision. Intelligent design theorists make no comments regarding the Bible or God, for they strongly hope for ID to be accepted as a legitimately scientific enterprise. But a recent federal court decision in Dover, Pennsylvania, classified ID as a form of creationism. Although ID supporters make no comment regarding the identity of the designer of the universe, the only logical candidate being God has resulted in the declaration of ID as a religious movement like creationism. Currently ID supporters continue their attempt to prove the inadequacies of contemporary evolutionary science, in concert with creationist strategy.

The third American viewpoint regards theology and science as working together as partners. Here the adherents do not find modern science in Genesis. They view the creation passages in Genesis as laying down a foundation for a theology of creation. And hence partnership supporters read Genesis 1 and 2 in a nonliteral way.

The final viewpoint, with science and theology as legitimate but independent enterprises, also results in no conflict. Many nonreligious scientists hold this position. But a number of Christian scientists also support this viewpoint, finding no modern science in Genesis as in the partnership position. Hence, these independence adherents also read Genesis in a nonliteral way.

The four American viewpoints depend at least partially on the literal or nonliteral way of interpreting biblical passages. The creationist and to a subtle extent the ID communities employ types of literalism, whereas a nonliteral understanding of creation in Genesis typifies the independence and partnership groups. Awareness of the Genesis and scientific sources of information and their interpretations constitutes the first step in approaching the creation-evolution conflict.

Two factors lead many Christians to their viewpoints. First, faithfulness to the intent of biblical texts such as Genesis 1 requires it to be read literally, except when the passage clearly calls for a nonliteral reading, as for a parable. The second factor involves the consistent elevation of creation in Genesis 1 over that found in Genesis 2:4-25, which is ignored or considered to be a subcategory in relation to the first account. Some Christians attempt to reconcile what, at first glance appears to be a number of important differences between the two accounts.

The primeval prologue of Genesis, chapters 1–11, parallels many other ancient Near Eastern writings. In particular, creation in Genesis 1 has the same form, subject matter and events as in a number of ancient pagan creation stories. However, the Genesis 1 account stands in stark contrast to these other accounts in that it describes an excellent planned creation carefully carried out by a monotheistic and universal God who treats humans as the pinnacle of creation. In contrast, the stories of the Hebrew's ancient neighbors depict creation as the result of conflict under the direction of a number of pagan beings who were using humans as slaves to carry out the menial work of creation.

Before the publication of Darwin's *The Origin of Species* in 1859, Christians generally read creation in Genesis in a literal way, for little or no scientific or historical evidence existed to challenge it. But the scientific and technological advances of the past 150 to 200 years have brought this reading into question.

Science, in contrast to the literal understanding of Genesis, reads in the universe and the earth a narrative of beginnings that has proceeded through billions of years, 13.7 billion years for the universe, 4.5 billion for our earth and about 3 billion years for life forms on earth. Primitive life developed into animal life over millions of years and, some thirty thousand years ago, into humans, all from a common ancestor. The entire process unfolds in the scientific account without any reference to the existence of a Creator God. Scientific and technological developments from the seventeenth century to the present have contributed to the current scientific picture. These include contributions from earth science, biological science, physics and cosmology. Christians who read Genesis literally reject this science, regarding it as a faulty, godless and anti-Christian enterprise. Some have made significant efforts to establish the earth as thousands and not billions of years old and to characterize evolutionary schemes as incomplete and erroneous.

The choice in the minds of many Christians is faithful (literal) Bible reading versus atheistic science. Two mistaken ideas underlie this choice. Faithful Bible reading does not always imply a literal reading, and science as a whole should not be classified as atheistic but rather as *methodologically* naturalistic, not *metaphysically* naturalistic.

INTERPRETATION OF SCIENTIFIC DATA

Here we present an outline of the current state of scientific work on beginnings in the form of scientific conclusions derived from the data rather than simply presenting the primary data. This is similar to the initial theological step in reading the Bible in the reader's own language rather than in ancient Hebrew for the Old Testament or in Greek for the New Testament. Working with and interpreting original data, whether biblical sources or scientific data, requires some specialized experience.[3]

Since the biblical book of Genesis addresses creation from before the beginning to just beyond the appearance of humanity, the following scientific sketch follows a similar timeline of important events.

No definitive scientific understanding exists of the universe before the big bang since no accelerator experiments can produce sufficient energy to probe that era. A number of proposals present various scenarios, but no evidence supports any of these.

Approximately 13.7 billion years ago, a cosmic fireball appeared from what seemed to be nothing. In fact, nothing for which we have evidence existed beforehand, not even space or time. Cosmologists (scientists who study the development of the universe) have determined the universe's age with an uncertainty of 0.12 billion years, an uncertainty of less than 1 percent. Our universe began as a cosmic fireball, not a few thousand years, not hundreds of thousands, not hundreds of millions, not even a few billion years ago, but 13.7 thousand

---

[3]The following is a partial list of scientific sources available for further reading, including information for this discussion: Eric J. Chaisson, *Cosmic Evolution* (Cambridge, Mass.: Harvard University Press, 2001); Peter Coveney and Roger Highfield, *The Arrow of Time* (New York: Fawcitt Columbine, 1990); Willem Drees, *Beyond the Big Bang* (LaSalle, Ill.: Open Court, 1990); John Gribben, *The Birth of Time* (New Haven, Conn.: Yale University Press, 1999); Robert Jastrow, *Red Giants and White Dwarfs* (New York: Norton, 1990); Stephen Hawking, *A Brief History of Time* (New York: Bantam, 1998); Michael Ruse, ed., *The Philosophy of Biology* (Amherst, N.Y.: Prometheus, 1998); John Maynard Smith and Eörs Szathmáry, *The Origins of Life* (Oxford: Oxford University Press, 1999); The Universe Adventure, Lawrence Berkeley National Laboratory Physics Division (August 2007) <http://theuniverse adventure.org>; The Big View, ed. Thomas Knierim (August 2009) <www.thebigview .com>; and various Wikipedia articles.

million years ago. An unimaginably enormous amount of energy, enough to produce all of the matter in the universe, was released in this infinitesimally small initial cosmic fireball. Except for the first minuscule fraction of a second after the big bang, cosmologists think they know rather well how the universe developed subsequently. Cosmologists conclude that our universe changed very rapidly during the first second of its existence. A number of epochs took place during that time. In the Planck epoch, the fundamental forces (electromagnetism, weak nuclear force, strong nuclear force and gravitation), all with the same strength, were probably united into one force. Next, during the grand unification epoch, gravity began to separate from the other three, and physics could be described by a grand unification theory. In that first second, the physics of the early universe continued to separate into the forces we observe today. In the electroweak epoch, the universe "cooled" to about 10^{28} degrees K, at which time the electroweak (electromagnetic and weak nuclear) force separated. This triggered a period of cosmic inflation as the universe expanded by the enormous factor of 10^{27}. After the end of this inflationary epoch, the universe was filled with a quark-gluon (building blocks of fundamental particles) plasma. As the quark epoch begins, a more certain understanding of the early universe replaces speculation by cosmologists. During this epoch, all the fundamental particles acquired a mass and all the four fundamental forces separated. In the hadron (heavy fundamental particles) epoch, the quark-gluon plasma cooled enough for the formation of hadrons, including familiar particles like protons and neutrons. All of this amazing activity occurred in the first second of the universe's life following the big bang.

Near the end of the first second, many hadrons had been annihilated, leaving leptons (light fundamental particles like electrons) and anti-leptons as the dominant types of particles in the universe. At the end of the universe's first three minutes, its temperature had dropped to the point where production of lepton/anti-lepton pairs ceased, followed by lepton/anti-lepton annihilation until there was only a small residue of leptons. This epoch ended with the completion of the formation of all of the universe's protons and neutrons.

The temperature of the universe continued to fall, allowing protons and neutrons to combine to form the light nuclei hydrogen and helium through the process of nuclear fusion. This continued until about twenty minutes after the big bang, and during this time the temperature and density of the universe fell to the point where fusion could no longer take place spontaneously.

After the end of the lepton epoch, photons (e.g., gamma rays and particles of light) dominated the energy content of the universe. These photons interacted with protons, electrons and nuclei, with the cooling electrons (at a temperature of about 2000 degrees K —still rather warm) beginning to be captured by light nuclei, forming neutral light atoms. This allowed the photons to begin to travel freely, and the universe became transparent. Remnants of this light can be observed today as the cosmic microwave background, giving cosmologists a picture of the universe at the end of this epoch.

At 300 million years beyond the big bang, gravitational attraction between denser regions of visible and dark matter began to cause atoms to coalesce, forming the first stars and galaxies. It took a billion years for galaxies to develop, and then 10 billion years for planets to appear around suitable stars.

Objects on the scale of our solar system formed approximately 5 billion years ago and our planet earth about 4.5 billion years ago. Approximately 3 billion years ago atoms first formed complicated molecules that could self-replicate, resulting in the first primitive microscopic life on our earth. Not until 30,000 years ago (or over 13 thousand million years after the big bang) did the human species come into existence.

Cosmologists for the most part agree on this timeline, although not all the details are known regarding exactly when or how these events came about. However, scientists working in these fields of investigation are confident that such details are worth pursuing, and based on a rich history of scientific successes, most scientists anticipate that more and more details will likely be understood as this enterprise of science moves forward.

Scientists cannot give a definitive prediction about the eventual fate of the universe. Among the possibilities include the big freeze, in which the universe reaches a high entropy state with little useful energy left. The temperature of the entire universe falls to approximately 10 degrees K (about -450 degrees F; very very cold). Under this possibility, eventually no life will exist anywhere in the universe. The big crunch refers to the time when the universe stops expanding and then ultimately contracts to its size just after the big bang, creating another big bang of enormous energy release. Again, there also can be no possibility for life after the crunch. In the big rip, all matter in the universe, from stars and galaxies to atoms and subatomic particles, is torn apart by the expansion of the universe to an infinite size. No life survives.

The consequence of any of these three possibilities (and others) as seen by scientists dooms the physical universe to a bad ending, including our earth, with everything either destroyed or becoming inert. This eventual dismal outcome depresses many scientists, but Christians know the story does not end here.

Because our minds have a hard time grasping both the infinitesimal and the enormous spans of time involved in the formation of the universe, it may be helpful to think of an outline of cosmic history in terms of two twenty-four-hour days. Imagine shrinking the history of our universe so that it fits into a forty-eight-hour period of time. Doing so results in the following timeline.

- The big bang occurs at midnight on the first of the two days.
- Light atoms form in the first six seconds.
- It takes about 3.25 hours on the first day for the first galaxies to appear.
- The earth is formed at approximately 11:00 a.m. on the second day.
- The first microscopic life on earth develops at around 2:00 p.m. on the second day.

• At long last, the human species comes into existence one-third of a second before the stroke of midnight on the second day.

SUMMARY

This chapter has included creation from Genesis 1 and 2 as the theological source, along with an outline of the current story as told today by scientists. Each refers to a set of valid information, but these and their interpretations differ. The creation-evolution conflict arises from the incompatible deductions originating in Genesis 1 and 2 and the scientific conclusions on beginnings. This has left many serious Christians in a quandary. Can one remain faithful to a Christian theological heritage but at the same time give due respect to the efforts of the many scientists who have contributed to our scientific understanding? And in particular, how should we regard contemporary evolutionary biology, since evolution seems to be contrary to the teachings of our Bible?

Our next task is to note some important characteristics of theology and science, characteristics that directly aid the analysis of the conflict. Their awareness and understanding will constitute a step in the movement toward its resolution.

2

Characteristics of Theology and Science Relevant to the Conflict

IN THIS CHAPTER, GERMANE CHARACTERISTICS of theology and science are noted. Knowledge of these will aid in the understanding of the roles that theology and science can play in bringing a satisfactory and truthful conclusion to the science-faith conflict. These characteristics fall under a set of similar categories, yet significant differences exist between these two enterprises.

First, the fundamental nature and foundation of theology and science are considered. This examination includes the source of knowledge and methods of knowing for each. Second, we examine the role of common sense in each enterprise and find that properties of the universe and theological truth go well beyond our limited direct experience and common sense. Third, the scope of valid applicability or limitations will be delineated for each, followed fourth by pointing out the necessity of employing systematic interpretive processes for each. Last, the possibility of theology or science legitimately informing the other in interpretation will be considered.

A number of the ideas in this chapter have been elegantly presented by John Polkinghorne in chapters three and four in his book

Serious Talk.[1] The current chapter has been influenced by Polkinghorne's work but also contains an expansion of his discussions in a
number of cases.

A note regarding discussions of the scientific characteristics—the
word *physics* occasionally replaces *science,* since physics encompasses
a wide range of science and the physicist/coauthor's professional experience with physics results sometimes in more familiarity with
physics than with generic science.

FUNDAMENTAL NATURE OF THEOLOGY AND SCIENCE

Christian theology seeks truth and, like science, wants to offer a
truthful understanding of the universe and all that occurs in that
universe. But theology differs from science in the type of questions it
addresses, questions that ask *why* rather than *how* of science. Hence,
theology investigates important topics unavailable to scientific investigation, topics such as God, love, purpose, destiny, the eschaton and
life after death.

Any search for understanding or any rational inquiry requires a
method of investigation appropriate to the nature of the reality being
investigated. Scientific investigations use the empirical experimental
method, wonderfully suited to investigations of the impersonal physical world. In these inquiries the scientist freely chooses a testable
hypothesis and an experimental strategy, and then performs an investigation to test the hypothesis in a manner the scientist deems
most appropriate. However, upon entering the realm of the theological and the personal, the experimental method used in science no
longer fits the investigation. Theological inquiry indeed has an element of discovery in it, but one should not attempt to manipulate
God or put God to the test. In healthy personal relationships, one
person does not put another person to the test. Furthermore, the
complexity of theological inquiry compared to that of scientific investigation many times results in a diversity of conclusions or opin-

[1]John Polkinghorne, *Serious Talk—Science and Religion in Dialogue* (Valley Forge,
Penn.: Trinity Press International, 1995).

ions. But these difficulties should not deter the inquirer from the delicate and essential task of seeking truth about people, about God and about the universe and seeking a proper personal relationship to all three.

Over the centuries the Christian church has used some combination of Scripture, tradition, reason and experience to inform its theological thinking. *Scripture* plays the primary and indispensable role in theology. It includes a record of those crucial historical events through which God has most clearly revealed himself to people. Scripture plays an essential role but is not the entirety of God's revelation. Creation also reveals God, but God is supremely known through the life and resurrection of the incarnate Christ. We hold a very high view of Scripture and see the Bible as the foundational source for the understanding of God, ourselves, our neighbors, the universe and our relationship to each. We affirm the words of Paul in 2 Timothy 3:14-17:

> But you must remain faithful to the things you have been taught. You know they are true, for you know you can trust those who taught you. You have been taught the holy Scriptures from childhood, and they have given you the wisdom to receive the salvation that comes by trusting in Christ Jesus. All Scripture is inspired by God and is useful to teach us what is true and to make us realize what is wrong in our lives. It corrects us when we are wrong and teaches us to do what is right. God uses it to prepare and equip his people to do every good work.

Over the years, a number of theological groups and councils have worked hard to understand and express the relationship between faith and Scripture and the place of the Bible in the life of the Christian. A group of evangelical leaders produced the Chicago Statement on Biblical Inerrancy at a summit conference held in Chicago in the fall of 1978. This congress wrote three major statements, one on biblical inerrancy (1978), one on biblical hermeneutics (1982) and a final statement on biblical application (1986). The Chicago Statement contains a preface, "A Short Statement," and then "19 Articles of Affirmation and Denial."[2] In the preface, the writers express their understanding of the importance of Scripture to faith:

> The authority of Scripture is a key issue for the Christian Church in this and every age. Those who profess faith in Jesus Christ as Lord and Savior are called to show the reality of their discipleship by humbly obeying God's written Word. To stray from Scripture in faith or conduct is disloyalty to our Master. Recognition of the total truth and trustworthiness of Holy Scripture is essential to a full grasp and adequate confession of its authority.
>
> The following Statement affirms this inerrancy of Scripture afresh, making clear our understanding of it and warning against its denial.

In the Articles of Affirmation and Denial, the writers address particular concerns regarding Scripture, as illustrated in the following portions:

Article VIII
We affirm that God in His Work of inspiration utilized the distinctive personalities and literary styles of the writers whom He had chosen and prepared.

We deny that God, in causing these writers to use the very words that He chose, overrode their personalities.

Article X
We affirm that inspiration, strictly speaking, applies only to the autographic text of Scripture, which in the providence of God can be ascertained from available manuscripts with great accuracy.

Article XI
We affirm that Scripture, having been given by divine inspira-

---

[2]Carl F. H. Henry, *God, Revelation and Authority* (Waco, Tex.: Word, 1979), 4:211-19.

tion, is infallible, so that, far from misleading us, it is true and reliable in all matters it addresses.

Article XVIII
We affirm that the text of Scripture is to be interpreted by grammatico-historical exegesis, taking account of its literary forms and devices, and that Scripture is to interpret Scripture. We deny the legitimacy of any treatment of the text or quest for sources lying behind it that leads to relativizing, dehistoricizing, or discounting its teaching, or rejecting its claims to authorship.

The Fuller Theological Seminary statement of faith includes a statement on Scripture that is a bit more concise:

Scripture is an essential part and trustworthy record of the divine self-disclosure. All the books of the Old and New Testaments, given by divine inspiration, are the written Word of God, the only infallible rule of faith and practice. They are to be interpreted according to their context and purpose and in reverent obedience to the Lord who speaks through them in living power.

We agree with these statements and join a wide range of Christian believers in affirming the essential role the Bible plays in Christian faith and theology. However, a problem can arise as one tries to read the Bible faithfully, for the Bible does not contain matter-of-fact accounts that clearly relate to us in the twenty-first century. Just as the data from scientific investigations must be interpreted to provide an accurate understanding of the implications of the data, the same must be done with Scripture. The biblical "data" (the words of Scripture) must be interpreted, as Article XVIII of the Chicago Statement indicates. Biblical interpretation (but not the original words of the Bible) may even undergo change or correction in the light of continuing experience and further reflection. This role of *tradition*—the record of insights of the worshiping, believing, studying and thinking Christian community of believers (the church)—benefits the church as it attempts to understand, incorporate and follow the words of Holy Scripture.

The church in its concern and pursuit of truth must be prepared to employ critical *reason* as Christian thinkers try to develop a coherent and consistent scriptural voice, especially when more than one voice addresses a given topic. Christian theology needs to pay attention to any source of knowledge that can add relevant information to an issue under consideration. Part of this, derived from *experience,* may come from sources other than Scripture (e.g., from scientific investigations). Christian theology must at least be aware of and acknowledge legitimate and relevant data that come from this source.

As we begin to address the character of science, Richard Carlson will share some personal observations regarding the scientific mind. He has worked with many nuclear-physics colleagues on research projects in laboratories in the United States, Canada, Sweden and South Africa. The projects have involved rather complex experiments, data analysis and theoretical calculations. Typical qualities of these colleagues include a passion for the research, complete scientific honesty and some fear, a fear that the conclusions drawn from the research might be wrong. For even after we make our best efforts, the possibility exists that the outcomes do not meet the criteria of excellence. Poorly done experiments may result in not receiving grant support or laboratory access for further research. Thus, not only our research team but the overwhelming majority of scientists put their very best efforts into their research, and scientists in general are scrupulously honest at least about their science. Those doing poor research may find their work no longer accepted for publication in research journals. And a scientist caught being intentionally dishonest will suffer exclusion from further research and the end of that scientist's career. Hence, scientific results published in peer-reviewed research journals almost invariably represent honest and competent best efforts. Results occasionally may be incorrect, but except in the rarest of cases, this is the result of a defect in the scientific study rather than fraud.

However, another matter arises when scientists go beyond science and engage in metascience or metaphysics. Metascience results when scientists write books or articles or produce TV programs for the general public containing pronouncements that go beyond that which science can rightfully address. For example, in the *Cosmos* series for TV, Carl Sagan presented marvelous science, but went beyond its legitimate purview in declaring that science comprises all that really matters, including religion, and that *nonscience* is *nonsense*. Carl Sagan did top-quality scientific work, but one should note the point at which he stops presenting science and starts to do metascience. Adhering to its self-imposed limitations characterizes legitimate science.

The nuclear research mentioned earlier has as its goal the attempt to "observe" nuclear reactions of interest. This implies dealing with time intervals of billionths of a second (actually not hard at all with modern electronic equipment) and studying nuclei of sizes that are about a ten-thousandth of a billionth of an inch. This is difficult because nuclei are one hundred thousand times smaller than an atom, which in itself is unobservable. Hence our eyes cannot directly "see" nuclear processes, but we are aware of their existence in an indirect way. The observations come in the form of little blips on an oscilloscope screen and numbers read from computers and various electronic detectors and counters. These numbers must be interpreted in relationship to the experimental method, with the goal of producing the results for which the research was planned and carried out. Next, these results are applied in the development of or comparison with a scientific theory dealing with these nuclear reactions. The quality of the experimental results depends on the skill of the research group. This process is typical of scientific research as the enterprise is complex and prone to error, so skill and care are essential in performing competent science. The successes of applied physics, from medical wonders such as proton cancer therapy to the marvels of computer technology and nanotechnology, are evidence of the skill and care usually present in this enterprise.

A different problem arises in historical science, the attempt to reconstruct the sequence of events that has led to some past or present condition. This can apply to the study of how the cosmos came into being and developed, or how the earth was formed and has changed, or how life on earth developed from nonlife to its current forms. Historical science does not have the advantage of laboratory science, where scientists do their investigations in an environment of their choosing and can repeat experiments time and time again until they think they have it right. Historical scientists only have the results from a single type of "experiment" with which to work, the developments in our universe. To make matters even more challenging, historical scientists must wrangle with the great antiquity of the universe, some 13+ billion years. But to their credit, those scientists have developed methods appropriate to their studies, reliable methods that many times can be validated by laboratory experiments.

Modern science, despite its methodological challenges, deserves to be taken seriously because of the character of its inquiry, a search for an understanding of the physical world in terms of experimentally accessible concepts. Two factors contribute to its success. First, it limits its inquiry to questions that can be explored in repeatable, controlled experiments that produce numbers. The hypothetical-deductive method—data → hypothesis → deduction—is the hallmark of modern science. Measurable data characterize scientific work, with perhaps the historical sciences as the exception in some cases. Second, the entire scientific enterprise rests on discovery and not construction from preconceived ideas or a desire for the data to turn out in a predetermined way. Often the physical world surprises scientists, and they must struggle hard to understand it. Many times scientists are challenged to go beyond current theories by what they learn in their investigations.[3]

In summary, science is solely interested in an understanding of the nature of the physical world in terms of experimentally accessible con-

---

[3]Polkinghorne, *Serious Talk*, p. 36.

cepts. For the most part, science is an honest and competent effort toward this end. Scientific results deserve our thoughtful consideration.

COUNTERINTUITIVE REALITY—TRUTH IS STRANGER THAN COMMON SENSE

Certain theological concepts elude the grasp of our finite minds and will not always fit perfectly into our expectations, sometimes called "common sense." Examples include the character of God, the meaning of the incarnation, the concept of Jesus Christ as fully human and fully God, the resurrection of Jesus, the idea of an afterlife along with heaven and hell, and the notion of miracles, to name just a few. Pitfalls exist here. Cutting God down to our human comprehension must be avoided, but so must the other extreme of invoking mystery as a lazy substitute for careful theological thought. We should embrace paradox or counterintuitive thought only when forced upon us by Scripture or our experience.

Christ as both fully God and fully human constitutes a paradox. Does it make sense that a member of the Godhead, the eternal Word, would voluntarily take the form of a servant and become one of us? The early church wrestled with such a question. It took four centuries for the patristic theologians, working with the evidence in Scripture and with sensitivity to the Holy Spirit, to come to a consensus in 451 at the Council of Chalcedon. There a statement was formulated expressing the essential character of our Lord Jesus Christ, given here in part.[4]

> Our Lord Jesus Christ, at once complete in Godhead and complete in manhood, truly God and truly man, consisting also of a reasonable soul and body; of one substance [*homoousios*] with the Father as regards his Godhead, and at the same time one substance with us as regards his manhood; like us in all respects, apart from sin; as regards his Godhead, begotten of the

---

[4]For example, see T. H. Bradley and F. W. Green, *The Oecumenical Documents of the Faith* (London: Methuen, 1950), pp. 85-235.

Father before the ages, but yet as regards his manhood begotten, for us men and for our salvation, of Mary, the Virgin, the God-bearer [*Theotokos*]; one and the same Christ, Son, Lord, Only-begotten, recognized IN TWO NATURES [*en dyo physesin*], WITHOUT CONFUSION [*asynchytōs*], WITHOUT CHANGE [*atreptōs*], WITHOUT DIVISION [*adiaretōs*], WITHOUT SEPARATION [*achōristōs*]; the distinction of natures being in no way annulled by the union, but rather the characteristics of each nature being preserved and coming together to form one person and subsistence.

This declaration defies common sense, and yet has not been modified since the Council in 451.

Further questions arise that defy human reason: Does it make sense that a person could walk on water? Or that this person would help a party host avoid a major foul-up by the odd method of turning water into the best of wine? Or that the same person could resuscitate a friend who had been dead for four days? Or that this person could restore sight to a man blind from birth? The journey of Christian faith requires a rethinking of what is possible, ultimately accepting paradox as truth when the evidence requires, just as the scientist must also sometimes do.

Many important characteristics of science far exceed our limited experiences. These represent only a small fraction of the complete description of all that exists in the physical universe. The majority of these phenomena are beyond our imaginations, so much so that sometimes the universe even appears to contradict itself. And the physical properties of the universe itself are difficult to grasp, with sizes varying from that of the microworld of the unobservable atom and nucleus to the unfathomable size of the universe. Masses of objects as well as speeds vary by enormous factors, factors that are hard to grasp. Yet all represent reality. In the microworld the counterintuitive quantum theory comes into play as does relativity theory (also counterintuitive) for phenomena with speeds near that of light.

In terms of our human experiences, the majority of the universe's physical phenomena do not fall under the category of common sense because we cannot directly observe them. Common sense is inadequate to account for all that is.

Consider the following simple example exhibiting one counterintuitive aspect of our physical universe. Imagine that Aunt Betty travels from Los Angeles to Boston with one stop to change planes, getting her connecting flight either in Chicago or Dallas. It must be one or the other airport, and certainly not some combination of both. An impossible scenario would be to find part of Aunt Betty at Chicago O'Hare and the rest of her at Dallas-Fort Worth. This conclusion is a result of observing people as they travel and is also a result of an application of the distributive law of classical logic. But if an electron replaces Aunt Betty, the same kind of logic no longer applies. This is because classical logic as worked out by Aristotle depends on the law of the excluded middle, since in this logic there is no middle term between (A) and (not A). This sharp either-or is removed by quantum theory, a theory that accounts for the behavior of very small entities like electrons. Quantum logic permits the probabilistic mixing together of possibilities that common sense would conclude are unmixable. An electron can be in a state of a mixture of here and not here, which yields a possibility undreamed of by Aristotle, sometimes here and there at the same time. The single electron, in traveling from Los Angeles to Boston, can go through both Dallas and Chicago at the same time, something that Aunt Betty could never do. This new kind of logic was worked out by quantum theorists in the twentieth century, and its strange ways have been verified by many experiments.

One of the consequences of the development of quantum theory has been to enlarge our imagination of what is possible. In the twentieth century, physicists learned that electrons sometimes behave like particles but at other times are spread out in a wavelike manner. This radical thought makes no common sense, for an electron as a particle is concentrated into a volume so small that its size cannot be measured, but an electron as a wave is spread throughout the entire universe. The complete description of an electron and all submicroscopic particles contains elements contrary to common sense. And yet, many experiments have demonstrated both aspects unambiguously. Light also exhibits the same kind of dual personality, sometimes as a spread-out wave and sometimes as a concentrated particle. Both properties are necessary in understanding the operation of such a simple piece of equipment as a point-and-shoot camera. Furthermore, all entities in the universe have this dual personality, called the wave-particle duality. And there is more. Even though an entity like an electron possesses both particle and wave properties, such an entity will never exhibit both properties at the same time. Reliable experimental investigations confirm these counterintuitive properties.

Another uncommon-sense aspect of the universe is found in the relativistic world of the unimaginably fast. For example, a spaceship moving faster and faster through space will begin to shrink in length and increase in mass as it reaches very high speeds[5] near the speed of light. This has been demonstrated through repeated investigations. And there is more uncommon sense. Clocks moving at speeds near that of light run more slowly than do clocks that remain near us. Ordinary light can be transformed into matter (into particles) and vice versa. At the beginning of the twentieth century, Albert Einstein developed his two theories of relativity, the special theory (1905) and the general theory (1915). The special theory stands as the best-ever affirmed scientific theory.

Humans cannot see either quantum-sized objects or objects with speeds close to that of light. No one has ever directly observed objects as they shrink and grow heavier near the speed of light, although those who have participated in many forms of physics research have observed the evidence that affirms such speeds.

The discussion here involves phenomena that are contrary to com-

---

[5]These are speeds near that of light—186,000 miles per second.

mon sense. And yet, there is reliable evidence that supports these strange conclusions. Contemporary physics delivers us from the tyranny of common sense. Common sense, the set of principles by which we understand the workings of the universe through our limited encounters with it, does not include much of how it operates. The physical world continues to surprise scientists as they investigate, probe and attempt to form a coherent picture of the entire cosmos. Both Christian theology and the physical universe encompass concepts and phenomena that extend beyond ordinary experience. A test of the truthfulness of a theological concept or a scientific conclusion cannot solely be, "I cannot imagine this" or "I don't understand this" or "I have never experienced this." One must do further examination before a final negative evaluation can rightly be made.

LIMITATIONS OF THEOLOGY AND SCIENCE

Christian theology deals with the most important issues of life in a nonempirical way. Theology's concern is with the personal rather than the impersonal of science. Theology cannot generally investigate questions more appropriate to science's strategy. Instead, Christian theology's interests focus on issues of purpose and value, questions about such things as love, God or ultimate destiny, questions that are inappropriate for scientific investigation.

Science is also a limited enterprise, as science consciously self-limits to those questions that can be empirically investigated, questions that are appropriate for laboratory investigation or historical investigation using the hypothetical-deductive method. Usually scientific investigations involve numbers, and the subject of an investigation goes under the designation of the impersonal "it." The most important questions of life are not the purview of science.

There are instances when contemporary science and Christian theology together give us a more complete picture than can be derived from either alone. For example, recently philosophers using the fine-tuning scientific cosmological, geological and physical data have constructed the best-ever philosophical argument for the existence of

God.[6] But generally, theology does not legitimately address scientific questions, and science does not address theological questions.

THE IMPORTANCE OF INTERPRETATION

The fourth characteristic of theology relates to the important role of systematic interpretation in Bible reading. Christian believers, no matter where they stand on the creation-evolution issue, whether they affirm positions of creationism, intelligent design, independence or partnership, all agree that the Bible is the ultimate authoritative reference for Christian faith. Disagreement over the meaning of creation in Genesis leads to the differing creation-evolution positions, even though the Bible serves as a main source for the Christian's investigation of this issue.

The use of the Bible requires careful reading and skillful interpretation. Any systematic interpretive method must include the reader's attempt to understand the intent of the biblical writer in delivering a given passage to its first hearers or readers. A biblical passage cannot mean something to twenty-first-century readers in contradiction to what it meant to those for whom it was first intended. One neglected factor in addressing the conflict between Christian faith and science is the need for careful biblical reading and interpretation of relevant passages. In fact, this may be the *key factor* for the Christian believer in resolving science-faith conflicts.

But the scientist also must take care in sifting through data acquired in a study in order to determine the relevant data and its meaning for the issue at hand. The data must be understood in terms of the context of the investigation, including the purpose of the scientific work, the scientific strategy, the method of data acquisition and its quality. Only after a careful evaluation can meaning be assigned to the data. In general, science involves obtaining numbers, and these numbers must be clearly understood in terms of how they

---

[6]For example, see Rodney D. Holder, *God, the Multiverse, and Everything* (Burlington, Vt.: Ashgate, 2004), and Michael J. Murray, ed., *Reason for the Hope Within*, foreword by Alvin Plantinga (Grand Rapids: Eerdmans, 1999).

were obtained. The successful scientist must determine which data acquired in a study reliably pertain to the question at hand. Many times these "good data" represent only a fraction of that collected.

THE CROSSTALK BETWEEN THE TWO ENTERPRISES

It must be recognized that theology and science have significantly different concerns and methodologies. One must be careful in advocating any influence that either enterprise should have on the other. Science cannot dictate a theological point of view, but in certain cases science might impose fences or limits on theological thought. In the same manner, theology cannot specify scientific thought or prescribe the results of a scientific investigation. But each may point out when the other exceeds its rightful limits. And each can provide helpful insight that may enhance the work of the other.

Polkinghorne[7] points out that a number of meaningful questions exist that interest science but that science is unable to answer. Some of these are metaquestions, such as what existed before the big bang or the significance of the deep intelligibility of the physical world and of its finely tuned anthropic fruitfulness.[8] Theology can give direction to science in these cases and can even suggest new scientific investigations such as a research study of the effectiveness of prayer. Theology can sometimes aid in going beyond science, working with science in making greater sense than can be gained using science alone. But in most cases theology and science act independently.

SUMMARY AND RELEVANCE FOR THE CONFLICT

In this chapter certain characteristics of both Christian theology and science have been discussed in terms of five similar categories for each. And yet they differ significantly. In relation to the thesis of this

---

[7]Polkinghorne, *Serious Talk*, p. 36.
[8]Finely tuned anthropic fruitfulness refers to the observation that our universe—its laws and physical constants, along with a number of properties of our earth and sun—are just what they must be in order that humanity (*anthropos*) would appear sometime during the development of the cosmos, our earth and its inhabitants. Scientifically, this is an amazing coincidence and a great surprise.

book, these characteristics play a role in addressing the creation-evolution conflict.

Diversity exists in theology, a more complex enterprise than science. However, both seek to give a rational account for what they rightfully address. The authors of this book affirm a high view of Scripture and agree with the Chicago Statement on Biblical Inerrancy and with Fuller Theological Seminary's statement of faith, and approach all biblical texts in a manner consistent with these. This includes application of grammatico-historical exegesis, awareness of literary styles and interpretation of Scripture by Scripture. The Chicago Statement also recognizes the personalities of the biblical authors to be reflected in their writing. These principles will be useful in the forthcoming biblical analyses, particularly in the analysis of the Genesis creation passages.

The high competency of the overwhelming majority of professional scientists suggests that the published results in their areas of competence should be taken seriously. One must be very careful before dismissing this scientific work. On the other hand, when scientists speak about matters that fall outside their areas of scientific expertise, one cannot assume that they can speak with the same authority. Essentially, all scientists do their professional work under the hypothetical-deductive method, resulting in a uniformity of approach to scientific problems. One should be careful before discounting scientists' current understanding of the long history of the universe and the earth and the development of life on our earth over the past three or so billion years. Of course any scientific principle for which there is clear contrary evidence calls for further scrutiny. If the scientific picture of beginnings proves to be incorrect, then major portions of contemporary physics, cosmology, earth science and biology would be brought into question, and scientific understanding would be pushed back to the seventeenth century. This possibility seems unlikely to us.

One must be careful in trying to understand certain theological concepts, and the same is true of many physical phenomena. Common sense does not always lead to valid conclusions. In both theology and science, paradox can arise. One simply cannot dismiss a theological principle or a scientific study merely because it defies our common sense. There must be appropriate evidence supporting the dismissal.

Both theology and science have limitations. Neither can address all that makes up our universe—relationships and phenomena. In short, theology tells us *why*, and science tells us *how*. Theology cannot give us information on the mechanisms of the operation of the physical universe, and science cannot give information on the most important questions of life, those of about God, ultimate destiny, personal relationships and love—questions that tell us *why* the universe and all in it are the way they are. Care must be exercised in applying theological data to scientific questions and vice versa.

The data of theology and science must be carefully interpreted, especially when investigating complex issues. This step, routinely a part of scientific investigations, is neglected many times in Bible reading. The most important source for theology resides in the words of the Bible. But it seems to us that not many Christians have been given instruction on how to read systematically and understand the Bible, especially passages out of which conflict arises. An important step in resolving a conflict is in applying a systematic interpretive method to relevant biblical passages. One such method will be offered in the next chapter.

Generally, Christian theology and science work as independent enterprises, and rightly so. On occasion, issues arise in which each can contribute to an investigation. But care must be exercised when doing so.

An issue to be pursued in this book relates to what appears to be scientific material in Genesis and science's contribution to the understanding of Genesis and to the solution of the conflict. We will discuss how the characteristics of both theology and science play into the understanding of creation in Genesis. The next step in trying to solve the conflict is to become aware of the necessity of systematic biblical interpretation.

3

Biblical Interpretation—
A Key Element in Resolving the
Creation-Evolution Conflict

THIS CHAPTER ARISES FROM OUR conviction of the importance of carefully interpreting the Bible and applying a good interpretive method to biblical passages that address creation. This is an important step in confronting the creation-evolution conflict, an issue not directly addressed in the Bible. In fact, applying careful biblical interpretation may be a compulsory factor in resolving the conflict. Two related topics, literary genre and the incarnational nature of the Bible, will conclude this chapter.

One hermeneutical method will be discussed here and then applied in the following three chapters to the principal biblical passages in which creation plays an important role. Examining all these passages will allow this biblical witness to contribute to the reconciliation of the conflict.

Inherent difficulties face the reader in understanding and applying the Bible, a book of the distant past. The Bible addresses cultures and historical situations far different from our own. Furthermore, the interpreter must pick from a number of different hermeneutical methods. A person reading the Bible always applies an interpretive

principle, for one cannot read any piece of literature in the absence
of one.

One goal of biblical hermeneutics must include the attempt of the
reader to understand the author's intent in writing a given passage for
his or her readers or hearers.[1] Careful completion of this step is necessary before a reader may be confident in applying the passage to a
current issue.

Biblical hermeneutics have been aided by progress over the years
in the theory of language. Nancey Murphy points out[2] that in the
modern period (seventeenth to mid-twentieth century) language was
understood to function in only one of two ways. In the referential (or
representative) aspect, language gets its meaning by describing facts
or objects. Here one reads words in a sentence as actually represent-
ing that being described; the descriptions and events are to be understood literally. The second, the expressivist aspect, refers to a kind of
second-class theory of language. Here language gains its meaning
because it expresses some inner attitude, feeling, or intention of the
speaker or writer. Language contains no factual meaning. In the
modern period, theology could adopt only one or the other aspect of
language since language at that time was understood as functioning
only in these two ways. The conservative church opted for the referential aspect (and one might ask, was there really any other choice?),
while the liberal church chose the expressivist. But neither version
alone can describe all dimensions of how language actually works.
Professor Murphy concludes that this left the conservative wing of
the Christian church (now the evangelicals or the fundamentalists)
with a theory of language that gave little choice other than to interpret all Scripture in a literal way except for portions clearly not intended to be so understood, such as the parables of Jesus or certain
poetic passages. When the choice was not clear, the faithful response

---

[1]Tremper Longman III, *Reading the Bible with Heart and Mind* (Colorado Springs: Nav-
Press, 1997), p. 85.
[2]Nancey Murphy, *Anglo-American Postmodernity: Philosophical Perspectives on Science,
Religion, and Ethics* (Boulder, Colo.: Westview, 1997), pp. 10-11.

required the passage to be understood literally. This theory of language still prevails for many Christians today. The discussion of a biblical hermeneutical method to follow will reflect a more nuanced understanding of language.

All contemporary approaches to biblical hermeneutics involve three main components: the author—the text—the reader. Each hermeneutical method shares two main goals, to get to what the text meant to its first hearers or readers and to aid the reader in formulating an appropriate understanding for today. All methods emphasize content and context, with each using a more highly developed approach to language than in the modern period. The following hermeneutical approach, one of many, combines the components of content, context and reader response.

CONTENT (EXEGESIS)

A number of steps are involved in determining the content of the text of interest, a process called exegesis.

1. The text in its original language, the ideal starting place, requires knowledge of that ancient language. The existence of only incomplete fragments of the original text of the New Testament further complicates the possibility of working with that text, although scholars have worked hard to combine the fragments into what appears to be a trustworthy Greek text, the Nestle-Aland version. The Hebrew Old Testament, *Biblia Hebraica Stuttgartensia,* is widely used by scholars.

2. The words chosen by the biblical writer also present problems to the interpreter, for the meanings of biblical words in Hebrew and Greek have undergone change since their original use. Fortunately, lexicons exist that trace these meanings over time.

3. The nuances of a particular grammatical construction may hold the key to understanding a passage, and thus a thorough knowledge of ancient grammar is essential.

4. Awareness of the syntax aids in determining the meaning of a unit

as a whole. This refers to all the interrelationships within a sentence, including those between words, phrases, clauses and even between sentences. Syntax includes compositional patterns, grammar and semantics.

In summary, determining the content involves producing an accurate translation of the biblical text into the language of the reader. Most readers of the Bible will not have the tools to do this and hence must depend on an available translation. For English language readers, there is a plethora of available modern translations that attempt to competently carry out the exegetical steps outlined above. It then falls on the reader to pick a translation for study. Our choice for this book, the New Living Translation, second edition, is one of a number of perfectly satisfactory translations.

CONTEXT

The accurate determination of the content of a text is a necessary, but not a sufficient, step many times for complete biblical interpretation. Awareness of the context of the passage in question constitutes another important component in understanding the author's motivation. The following steps aid in doing so.

1. Biblical authors chose a particular literary genre. Frequently, the identification of the genre of a passage plays a crucial role in the attempt to understand the author's intent. An expanded discussion of genre will be given later in this chapter.

2. Understanding the historical and cultural context is a necessary step in determining the purpose of a given passage. The historical setting in which the recipients found themselves possibly provided motivation and context for the biblical author as he reacted to his readers' situation. The culture of the recipients or the culture of their setting might have influenced the writing in dealing with a given situation.

3. The social or religious context addresses the use of the particular passage by its original recipients. The form of communication

(writing) was generally appropriate for the social or religious setting, and that form should be identified and its usage understood by the reader. For example, psalms were used by the people of Israel in worship.

4. Understanding the style, literary form or tone of the passage gives a clue to understanding what the author was trying to accomplish in that particular passage. His intent may be revealed by his attitude and emotions through the tone of the passage. Compare the apostle Paul's gentle attitude of approval shown toward the Philippian church in his letter to them with his harsh comments of criticism to the Galatians ("I am shocked. . . . Oh, foolish Galatians!" [Gal 1:6; 3:1]).

5. A biblical writer sometimes acted as an editor in using a number of sources for a passage or a book. The choice of sources may give a clue toward understanding the editor's intent in his decision to put the chosen sources together into the final form of the passage.

6. An additional principle of interpretation that applies especially to Bible study involves determining how a given passage compares with other passages that employ the same overall theme. The principle of comparing Scripture with Scripture assists in trying to get a full understanding of a passage. Considerations include how a given passage fits into the biblical book in which it is found, into its section of its testament and into the whole of Scripture.

READER RESPONSE (UPTAKE)

The final step can be stated simply. The hearer or reader must "get it," must understand the point of the passage and the author's motivation and message to his intended audience. The goal is thereby reached.

All these steps of interpretation put together constitute inductive Bible study. Both the older referential and expressivist aspects of language contribute to this more comprehensive approach, each having a role to play, but each in itself is wholly inadequate for biblical hermeneutics.

The time necessary to be careful and thorough must be invested, for the study of the Bible deserves such. One should not casually flip to a passage, read it, especially in isolation from other passages, and always expect to understand the author's purpose and message to the original audience. The understanding and application of a passage would be open to question when a person uses such a casual and short-cut approach, especially in reference to complex issues. This does not refer to truths that simply leap out of the Bible, but pertains to issues over which controversy has arisen within the church, issues such as the creation-evolution conflict.

GENRE—A FURTHER WORD

At this point we expand on the topic of genre, briefly mentioned without comment in the context section of this chapter. Its importance for biblical understanding motivates a further discussion. Earlier it was pointed out that an important ingredient in biblical interpretation includes the identification of the genre of a passage, the literary form or type of literary composition. As Ronald L. Giese Jr. writes in the introduction to the book *Cracking Old Testament Codes,* "Accurate interpretation hinges then on recognizing the genres used in the Bible to communicate God's revelation."[3]

Further, "the Bible has literary codes that reveal how authors were expressing the word of the LORD and what they intended to communicate. Understanding what these codes are and the significance of them will help keep readers from misinterpreting Scripture and will guide them into correct interpretation and application."[4]

The writer to the Hebrews in the New Testament recognized that the Old Testament contains a number of literary forms, as the opening verse in Hebrews declares in reference to the Old Testament era: "Long ago God spoke many times and in many ways to our ancestors

---

[3]Ronald L. Giese Jr., "Literary Forms of the Old Testament," in *Cracking Old Testament Codes,* ed. D. Brent Sandy and Ronald L. Giese Jr. (Nashville: Broadman & Holman, 1995), p. 14.
[4]Ibid., p. 2.

through the prophets" (Heb 1:1). Note the phrase "in many ways." John Feinberg raises the possibility "whether it is possible to communicate something without using genre." He replies to his own question: "The answer is no."[5] He goes on to declare, "God's revelatory acts . . . incorporate genre."[6] Finally, Feinberg states, "Anyone who thinks it is proper to discuss the manner or content of biblical revelation without appeal to the notion of genre is misguided."[7]

If these theologians are correct, and we believe they are, then the biblical reader not only must be alert to the use of different genres in the Bible but also must correctly identify the genre in the process of attempting to understand the meaning of a passage.

The Bible contains a variety of literary forms, each chosen carefully by the writer in a way that is consistent with the writer's purpose for a given passage. The forms include prose, poetry, narrative, parable, historical account, prophetic account, worship materials, wisdom literature and others. Examples of their use include giving praise or issuing complaint in worship in the psalms, proclaiming God's judgment in the prophets, pointing out the generally expected outcome of certain conduct in the proverbs, telling the story of God's chosen people in the historical books, dealing with certain crises in the apocalyptic passages, and teaching through Jesus' parables. Each type of biblical writing requires an appropriate literary form, particularly in the Old Testament.[8]

One reads a legal document differently from a mystery novel, a mystery novel differently from a want ad or the comics, and the account of the action on a bill in Congress differently from *Gulliver's Travels*. A reader expects the facts contained in an account of a scientific breakthrough to be literally true and accurate in the same way as a historical account of the explorations of Lewis and Clark. But we

---

[5]John Feinberg, "Literary Forms and Inspiration," in *Cracking Old Testament Codes,* ed. D. Brent Sandy and Ronald L. Giese Jr. (Nashville: Broadman & Holman, 1995), p. 49.
[6]Ibid., p. 57.
[7]Ibid., p. 58.
[8]Giese, "Literary Forms of the Old Testament," pp. 5-28.

don't expect the same of Milton's *Paradise Lost,* although the truth content may very well be more significant in *Paradise Lost* than in certain scientific or historical accounts.

The identification of the genre of a piece of literature generally requires little thought or analysis. This is the case for most contemporary writing. But the Old Testament was written two to four thousand years ago for an ancient culture markedly different from our Western culture. Here the identification of the literary form of a given biblical passage can be more complex. This applies to the two creation narratives of Genesis 1 and 2, as the determination of their genres, including their literalness or nonliteralness, is not immediately apparent. The sacred author formed his creation accounts in terms of the scientific and historical understandings of the ancient people of Israel. But possibly there is more to the genre identification for these passages than simply that of an ancient cosmology and historical account. The genre question for Genesis 1 and 2 will be discussed in detail in chapter six. In preparation for this analysis, we look next at the appropriateness of presenting truth using a nonliteral genre such as story or fantasy.

Many readers of this book were taught as children the truth of the Bible, including all of the stores therein. Only a rare parent or Sunday school teacher would deny this important idea. Children are taught both the truth of the Bible and the literal truth of its words. This turns out to be the appropriate procedure in many cases. However, it must be remembered that the Bible falls under the category of a literary work, the literary work that is the foundational source for Christian belief and faith. We wish to explore the possibility that certain passages in literary works in general and in the Bible in particular are significantly *more true when understood in a nonliteral way.* In certain cases, a writer will intentionally use the nonliteral genre of story or fantasy (sometimes called myth). This is done to convey truth in a more effective way than if the writing were *merely* factually accurate. The case will be made later that rather than factual accounts, Genesis 1 and 2 function for twenty-first-century Christians as *two different stories of creation,* stories that describe creation in the form of scientific and historical accounts as understood by the ancient people of Israel, but that are not historically and scientifically factually true by twenty-first-century standards. Truth underlies the two creation passages in the form of stories. At first glance, this suggestion may raise some eyebrows, and so next we examine the use of writing by Christian authors that could be classified as nonliteral truth.

The motivation for considering the possibility of story as a legitimate biblical genre originates in a problem that is encountered in the analysis of the Genesis 1 and 2 creation accounts. The possibility that these passages contain nonliteral truth must be considered. Please note that the authors of this book clearly affirm that the Bible does not deceive, for it tells the truth. The crucial issue here focuses on the identification of the genre the sacred writer used to tell the truth in Genesis 1 and 2.

We find that Jesus, many biblical writers and respected Christian authors use parable, metaphor, fantasy or story as their deliberately chosen means of proclaiming truth in a nonfactual form. The response by some Christians to these expanded ideas of biblical genre may go something like, "But if I can't believe this passage, what can I believe in the Bible?" This comment implies that declaring a biblical passage to be nonliteral implies that the passage is not a Holy Spirit–inspired passage. Some fear that this starts us down the slippery slope toward concluding that the Bible is not God's Word. We agree that this is a legitimate concern that requires some caution. But we do not want to cause the loss of anyone's faith, nor do we have the intention of casting any doubt on the trustworthiness of the Bible. Our motivation here is to help *clarify* the meaning of Genesis 1 and 2, and thereby obtain an understanding closer to that of the sacred author's intent, and hence draw closer to what God may want to teach twenty-first-century believers. A passage of Scripture correctly identified as written in a nonliteral genre is no less inspired than a passage using a literal genre.

Definition of **myth**. The term *myth* can raise concerns and confusion when used in regard to theology. In its general use (one might say its popular use) *myth* refers to stories that are fictional, and hence for the serious biblical user the word may carry a negative connotation. In his article "Myth," I. Howard Marshall points out that the term has four nuances, and any or all could apply in a given situation. Marshall defines these uses:

1. A myth may be a story which attempts to explain the origins of things without the use of modern historical and scientific investigation. Myth can thus be represented as pre-scientific thinking, and this may lead to a negative evaluation of it.

2. A myth may depict some aspect of human experience in the form of a story about the past. The story of an original "social contract" which expresses the structure of society by a fictitious example of "how it began" would be a myth of this kind.

3. A myth may be a story which is presented in terms of some symbolism and thus has a poetic or emotional appeal and is capable of reinterpretation in the light of fresh experiences. Some of the deepest feelings of people about the human predicament may find expression in mythical form.

4. The term is often used to refer to any kind of story which involves the gods or other supernatural actors.[9]

Marshall points out that the classification alone of a story as myth does *not* give judgment on its historical truth or falsity, just as a parable may or may not be historical. He writes that the important question about a myth is whether the point it makes is valid.[10] For example, a myth (not found in the Bible) might proclaim that after God created the world, he pronounced creation to be bad or defective because creation resulted from conflict in the Godhead. This

---

[9]I. Howard Marshall, "Myth," in *New Dictionary of Theology*, ed. Sinclair B. Ferguson, David F. Wright and J. I. Packer (Downers Grove, Ill.: InterVarsity Press, 1988), pp. 449-50.

[10]Ibid., p. 450.

myth would rightly be judged as invalid. Marshall further writes that myth is a well-recognized literary genre, with no inherent reason why the biblical writers should have avoided its use. "A myth may very well be valid even though its story is fictitious."[11] And finally Marshall makes the point that sometimes what is called mythical is really analogical or symbolical, especially when referring to God.[12]

Clearly Jesus extensively used the genre of myth, called parable in his teaching. Did a camel really go through the eye of a needle? Did a farmer actually scatter seeds among the four kinds of soil in his field? It would make more sense for a real farmer to sow his seeds only in what he judged to be the best soil. Rather than giving his audience a list of things to do and not do, or a straightforward discourse on the defects of Hebrew law, Jesus consistently chose parable as his teaching tool. Since parable was used by Old Testament wisdom teachers, by using parables Jesus was indirectly claiming to be a teacher in the wisdom tradition.[13] Parable was also the ideal genre for subjects beyond the comprehension of his audience. And he taught about things his audiences had not as yet experienced by comparing these new concepts to their everyday experiences. Jesus used these "false" stories (myths) to teach his audience theological truth. And he must have found this genre of parable, story or myth to be an effective means by which to convey his message.[14]

Examples of Christian myth. In addition to Jesus, a number of well-regarded Christian writers have used myth, story or fantasy in their writing as a means of effectively conveying truth. Among these are Madeleine L'Engle, C. S. Lewis and J. R. R. Tolkien.

Madeleine L'Engle. In *The Rock That Is Higher: Story as Truth,* L'Engle devotes an entire book to discussing the use of story. She carefully develops the concept that literal fact is not always the truth but that

---

[11]Ibid.
[12]Ibid., p. 451.
[13]Longman, *Reading the Bible with Heart and Mind,* pp. 195-96.
[14]Ibid.

story is sometimes the best avenue to tell the truth. She begins the chapter "Story as the Search for Truth" by declaring,

> For truth we can read Jesus. Jesus is truth. If we accept that Jesus is truth, we accept an enormous demand: Jesus is wholly God, and Jesus is wholly human. Dare we believe that? If we believe in Jesus, we must. And immediately that takes truth out of the limited realm of literalism.
>
> But a lot of the world, including the Christian world (sometimes I think especially the Christian world), is hung up on literalism, and therefore confuses truth and fact. . . . Is this rather general fear of story not so much a fear that the story is not true, as that it might actually be true?
>
> Karl Barth wrote that he took the Bible far too seriously to take it literally. Why is that statement frightening to some people? There is no way that you can read the entire Bible seriously and take every word literally.[15]

She turns to the Bible with this comment: "The Bible is not objective. Its stories are passionate, searching for truth (rather than fact), and searching most deeply in story. . . . There is still the common misconception, the illusion, that fact and truth are the same thing. No! We do not need faith for facts; we do need faith for truth."[16]

And then L'Engle goes on to recount how Jesus used story to tell truth:

> Jesus, the storyteller, told of a man who had a plank of wood in his eye and yet criticized another man for having a speck of dust in his eye. *"You hypocrite,"* he said, *"first take the plank out of your own eye, and then you will see clearly to remove the speck from your brother's eye."* This parable, like most of Jesus' stories, is true. Why must it be factual?[17]

---

[15]Madeleine L'Engle, *The Rock That Is Higher: Story as Truth* (Colorado Springs: Waterbrook, 1993), pp. 87, 88.
[16]Ibid., pp. 91-92.
[17]Ibid., p. 93.

L'Engle further writes, "We tell stories because they save us. . . . And how do we come to meaning and truth except through story? . . . The storyteller is a storyteller because the storyteller cares about truth, searching for truth, expressing truth, sharing truth."[18] Madeleine L'Engle sums up her attitude toward story near the end of the book: "Let's recover our story because we'll die without it. It's a life-giving story—this magnificent narrative we find in Scripture—if we are willing to read openly and to read all of Scripture, not just the passages selected to help us prove our point. . . . Jesus. The God who came to us and told us stories. How marvelous! Story reawakens us to truth, the truth that will set us free."[19]

C. S. Lewis. A safe guess is that many readers of this book have read C. S. Lewis's Chronicles of Narnia or The Space Trilogy or both. These books contain stunning imagery in terms of fantasy, story and myth, and in addition, they effectively tell theological truth. But are these stories factual? Can Narnia be located on any map of our world? There is no question of the existence of lions, but what about a particular lion named Aslan as depicted by Lewis? Did the children really pass through a wardrobe and into Narnia? It must be admitted that in terms of literal accuracy regarding actual places, people and animals, Lewis missed the mark. But we are not concerned that these narratives contain so much that is not factual and not true in the literal sense. Many Christians have read these stories to their children. Perhaps you, the reader, have done so. Why do we tell our children such "untruth"? We do so because these stories are both fascinating and at the same time effectively proclaim theological truth. We understand the genre of these accounts. And because we understand both the genre and the quality of their message, we deeply appreciate them for what they are.

Despite Lewis's extensive use of myth and story in his writing, he did not always think highly of myth. Before his conversion to Christianity, Lewis once told J. R. R. Tolkien that myths were "lies and

---

[18]Ibid., pp. 94, 102.
[19]Ibid., pp. 222-24.

therefore worthless, even though breathed through silver." "No," Tolkien replied, "They are not lies." Tolkien told Lewis that myths were the best way—and sometimes the only way—of conveying truths that otherwise could not be expressed in words. He explained that the story of Christ was the true myth at the center of history and at the very root of reality, and that the true myth of Christ was God revealing himself in the incarnation as the ultimate poet who was creating reality, the true myth. Thus paradoxically myth is revealed as ultimate realism. As a result of this conversation, Lewis's conception of Christianity changed in a way that resulted in his conversion.[20]

And so Lewis turned to story, to myth. After his conversion to Christianity, Lewis began to refer to myth in his writings in positive ways. In his essay "Myth Became Fact" (1944), Lewis writes,

> Now as myth transcends thought, Incarnation transcends myth. The heart of Christianity is a myth which is also a fact. The old myth of the Dying God, *without ceasing to be myth* comes down from the heaven of legend and imagination to the earth of history. It *happens*—at a particular date, in a particular place, followed by definite historical consequences. We pass from a Balder or an Osiris, dying nobody knows when or where, to a historical Person, crucified (it is all in order) *under Pontius Pilate*. By becoming fact it does not cease to be myth: that is the miracle.[21]

In the same essay Lewis goes on to write,

> Those who do not know that this great myth became Fact when the Virgin conceived are, indeed to be pitied. But Christians also need to be reminded . . . that what became Fact was a Myth, that it carries with it into the world of Fact all the properties of a myth. God is more than a god, not less; Christ is more

---

[20]Joseph Pearce and J. R. R. Tolkien, "Truth and Myth," *Lay Witness,* September 2001.

[21]C. S. Lewis, "Myth Became Fact," in *God in the Dock: Essays on Theology and Ethics,* ed. Warren Hooper (Grand Rapids: Eerdmans, 1967), pp. 66-67. Emphasis in original.

than Balder, not less. We must not be ashamed of the mythical radiance resting on our theology.[22]

In *The Pilgrim's Regress*, the first book Lewis published (1933) after his conversion, Lewis refers to myth in general:

Child, if you will, it is mythology. It is but truth, not fact: an image, not the very real. But then it is My mythology. The words of Wisdom are also myth and metaphor: but since they do not know themselves for what they are, in them the hidden myth is master, here it should be servant: and it is but of man's inventing. This is My inventing, this is the veil under which I have chosen to appear even from the first until now. For this end I made your senses and for this end your imagination, that you may see My face and live. What would you have? Have you not heard among the pagans the story of Semele? Or was there any age in our land when men did not know that corn and wine were the blood and body of a dying and yet living God?[23]

In the fantasy stories of the Narnia and Space Trilogy series, Lewis brilliantly uses myth to point out important facets of Christianity in ways that are intelligible to children as well as to adults.

J. R. R. Tolkien. J. R. R. Tolkien, author of *The Lord of the Rings,* devoted a major portion of his professional life to creating narrative in the form of fantasy and myth, or as he put it, he devoted his life to fairy stories. He discusses reasons for having chosen this genre in his book *The Silmarillion* and his essay "On Fairy-Stories."[24]

Tolkien knew that theologians were wary of the mythological imagination. Theology generally opted for so-called objective reality, the referential use of language, and aligned with the modern scientific method. This tended to transcend the creativity of fantasy. But Tolkien noted that the gospel itself remains a story exhibiting many

---

[22]Ibid., p. 67.

[23]C. S. Lewis, *The Pilgrim's Regress* (Grand Rapids: Eerdmans, 1958), p. 171.

[24]For example, see J. R. R. Tolkien, *The Silmarillion* (Boston: Houghton Mifflin, 1999), p. xv.

varieties of imagination. He comments on such matters in "On Fairy-Stories" as he was completing *The Lord of the Rings* near the outbreak of World War II. In Tolkien's mind, the genre of fairy stories (fantasy) is stronger and more creative and more adult than ordinarily thought of by most people. Tolkien writes,

> The realm of fairy-story is wide and deep and high and filled with many things: all manner of beasts and birds are found there; shoreless seas and stars uncounted; beauty that is enchantment, and an ever-present peril; both joy and sorrow are as sharp as swords. In that realm a man may, perhaps, count himself fortunate to have wandered, but its very richness and strangeness tie the tongue of a traveler who would report them.[25]

Tolkien addresses a surprisingly complex question, What is a fairy story? He writes that these stories are about Faërie, the realm or state in which fairies have their being. It is a realm of enchantment that transmutes our sense of reality.[26] In his words, "A 'fairy-story' is one which touches on or uses Faërie, whatever its own main purpose may be: satire, adventure, morality, fantasy."[27]

Tolkien claims that something is missing from a purely rational scientific approach to the universe, and that fairy stories and fantasy are, in addition to a scientific approach, a legitimate path to truth.[28] He ends his essay in an epilogue as he sums up his understanding of true fairy story and fantasy:

> The peculiar quality of the "joy" in successful Fantasy can thus be explained as a sudden glimpse of the underlying reality or truth. It is not only a "consolation" for the sorrow of this world, but a satisfaction, and an answer to that question, "Is it true?" The answer to this question that I gave at first was (quite

---

[25]J. R. R. Tolkien, "On Fairy-Stories," in *Tree and Leaf* (London: HarperCollins, 2001), p. 3.
[26]Ibid., p. 9.
[27]Ibid., p. 10.
[28]Ibid., pp. 13-17.

rightly): "If you have built your little world well, yes: it is true in that world." . . . But in the "eucatastrophe"[29] we see in a brief vision that the answer may be greater—it may be a far-off gleam or echo of *evangelium* in the real world. The use of this word gives a hint of my epilogue. It is a serious and dangerous matter. It is presumptuous of me to touch upon such a theme; but if by grace what I say has in any respect any validity, it is of course only one facet of a truth incalculably rich: finite only because the capacity of Man for whom this was done is finite.

I would venture to say that approaching the Christian Story from this direction, it has long been my feeling (a joyous feeling) that God redeemed the corrupt making-creatures, men, in a way fitting to this aspect, as to others, of their strange nature. The Gospels contain a fairy story, or a story of a larger kind which embraces all the essence of fairy stories. They contain many marvels—peculiarly artistic, beautiful, and moving: "mythical" in their perfect, self-contained significance; and among the marvels is the greatest and most complete conceivable eucatastrophe. But this story has entered History and the primary world; the desire and aspiration of sub-creation has been raised to the fulfillment of Creation. The birth of Christ is the eucatastrophe of Man's history. The Resurrection is the eucatastrophe of the story of the Incarnation. This story begins and ends in joy. It has pre-eminently the "inner-consistency of reality." There is no tale ever told that men would rather find was true. . . . Because this story is supreme; and is true, Art has been verified. God is the Lord, of angels, and of men—and of elves. Legend and History have met and fused.[30]

---

[29]The term *eucatastrophe* has been defined by Tolkien earlier in this essay as the "good catastrophe" occurring with a sudden and joyous turn at the most desperate juncture in the story. Tolkien says that "the eucatastrophe tale is the true form of fairy-tale, and its highest function. . . . In its fairy-tale—or otherworld—setting, it is a sudden and miraculous grace: never to be counted on to recur" (ibid., pp. 68-69).

[30]Ibid., pp. 71-73.

Tolkien's lifelong creation of fantasy resulted from his conviction that this genre was the most effective method for conveying truth. With fantasy, the reader or listener need not pay close attention to the facts, and as a result can concentrate on the real point of the story. The contemporary theologian Grant T. Osborne summarizes the use of nonliteral genres in the Bible by identifying the biblical use of metaphor. In his book *The Hermeneutical Spiral,* he writes,

> In fact, most theological concepts in Scripture are essentially metaphorical. This is because eternal truths cannot be expressed in human, temporal language with exactness. Metaphors are not only the best way to depict such concepts but they are the way God has chosen to express himself in Scripture. Moreover, it is not correct to intimate that metaphors by nature are vague or dispensable. The answer is a proper understanding of metaphor as a theological tool and a proper delineation of its referential nature.[31]

Osborne writes further,

> "Although metaphors are not literally 'true,' there is no reason to suppose that truth has to be literal."
>
> In other words, metaphors communicate themselves indirectly but should not be unduly contrasted with literal language, as if an indirect relation to reality (metaphorical) is less meaningful than a direct relation to reality (literal). No term is either literal or metaphorical: context will tell us whether a word is used literally or metaphorically; the key point is that in both cases meaning is understood. In short, the "truth" of an utterance does not depend upon its literal nature.[32]

In summary, truthful writing, particularly biblical writing (which

---

[31]Grant R. Osborne, *The Hermeneutical Spiral: A Comprehensive Introduction to Biblical Interpretation* (Downers Grove, Ill.: InterVarsity Press, 2006), pp. 387-88.

[32]Ibid., p. 389; Timothy Binkley, "On Truth and Probability in Metaphor," in *Philosophical Perspectives on Metaphor,* ed. Mark Johnson (Minneapolis: University of Minnesota Press, 1981), p. 149.

we maintain is truthful), does not always appear in terms of literally expressed concepts. The nonliteral genres of story, fantasy, myth and metaphor have been applied effectively and truthfully by faithful Christian authors and by biblical writers in certain places. In due course the suggestion will be made that the two creation accounts in Genesis 1 and 2 fall under the category of truthful nonliteral writing in terms of contemporary standards, and this recognition will be an important step in resolving the creation-evolution conflict.

A NOTE ON THE CHARACTER OF THE BIBLE—INSPIRED AND INCARNATIONAL

Peter Enns's recent book, *Inspiration and Incarnation: Evangelicals and the Problem of the Old Testament,* offers a thoughtful perspective on the character of the Old Testament and the Bible in general. Enns points out that one should look at evidence external to the Bible and account for this data, "while at the same time having a vibrant, positive view of Scripture as God's word."[33] Many Christians find a problem with the Old Testament. The first eleven chapters of Genesis, and in particular the two creation narratives, have a clear connection with the literature of ancient Israel's neighbors. This will be discussed further in chapter seven, devoted to a study of the two creation passages in Genesis 1 and 2. For now we affirm this observation and will think about its implications. The question arises of the status of the Old Testament as God's Word. Does the Old Testament really stand apart as unique when compared to this pagan literature of the ancient Near East? Or does the Old Testament simply reflect the ancient world in which it was produced? If the Old Testament is truly the Word of God, why does it fit so nicely with this pagan literature?[34]

Peter Enns writes that this question can be answered in a very satisfactory way by looking at our Lord Jesus Christ and recalling the declaration that Jesus Christ is both fully God and fully human. The question

---

[33]Peter Enns, *Inspiration and Incarnation: Evangelicals and the Problem of the Old Testament* (Grand Rapids: Baker Academic, 2005), p. 15.
[34]Ibid., pp. 15-16.

of Jesus' nature was settled at the Council of Chalcedon in 451, where the patristic theologians agreed that Jesus Christ is both fully God and fully human. The church has been satisfied with the Chalcedon work ever since, and the authors of this book affirm this creedal statement. Enns points out that Jesus, being both God and human, is not half-God and half-human, and not sometimes one and sometimes the other. And Jesus is not essentially one and only apparently the other. Jesus is indeed fully God and fully human simultaneously.[35]

At this point there is nothing really new here, but then Enns turns his attention to the Bible. Enns's insightful thesis suggests an analogy between Jesus as God and human and the Bible as a fully divine book but at the same time a fully human book. Jesus, God with us, in his earthly life was born a real Jew to Jewish parents, was raised in first-century Palestine and immersed himself in the culture of his Jewish homeland.[36] In his human, adult life, Jesus did what other Jews did; he ate, slept, went fishing, attended weddings, visited his home, enjoyed dinner parties, prayed and attended synagogue. But he also showed convincing evidence of his divinity. Enns points out that the same is true with the Bible. He writes,

> It [the Bible] belonged in the ancient worlds that produced it. It was not an abstract, otherworldly book, dropped out of heaven. It was *connected to* and therefore *spoke to* those ancient cultures. The encultured qualities of the Bible, therefore, are not extra elements that we can discard to get to the real point, the timeless truths. Rather, precisely because Christianity is a historical religion, God's word reflects the various historical moments in which Scripture was written. God acted and spoke in history. As we learn more and more about that history, we must gladly address the implications of that history for how we view the Bible, that is, what we should expect from it.[37]

---

[35]Ibid., p. 17.
[36]Ibid.
[37]Ibid., pp. 17-18. Emphasis in original.

Enns calls this way of thinking about the Bible an *incarnational analogy*. By this term he means that Christ's incarnation is analogous to what he calls the Bible's incarnation. The question Enns raises is "How does Scripture's full humanity and full divinity affect what we should expect from the Scripture?"[38]

Enns contends that if the Bible is fully incarnational in much the same way as Jesus, then the human dimension of Scripture is a crucial part of "what makes Scripture Scripture." But he points out that this human element of Scripture causes problems. For some, it makes the Bible seem less "Bible-ish."[39] And, among the human elements that are clear in the creation accounts of Genesis are the parallels of these accounts with the creation myths of Israel's ancient Near Eastern neighbors. But Enns contends that precisely this feature demonstrates to us "that the Bible, at every turn, shows how 'connected' it is to its own world is a necessary consequence of God incarnating himself."[40]

Enns summarizes the theme of his book by this rather extended statement,

> That the Bible bears an unmistakable human stamp does *not* lead to the necessary conclusion that it is *merely* the words of humans rather than the word of God. To these who hold such a position the question might be asked, "How *else* would you have expected God to speak? In ways wholly *disconnected* to the ancient world? Who would have understood him?"
>
> And to those who fear the human stamp as somehow dirtying the Bible, marring its perfect divinity, I say, "If you wouldn't say that about Jesus (and you shouldn't), don't think that way about the Bible. Both Christ and his word are human through and through." In fact, it is precisely by having the Son become human that God demonstrates his great love. Is it so much of a

---

[38]Ibid.
[39]Ibid.
[40]Ibid., p. 20.

stretch, then, to say that the human nature of Scripture is likewise a gift rather than a problem?[41]

In summary, Enns suggests that God's gift to his first peoples, the ancient people of Israel, was God's speaking meaningfully to them in terms that they could understand. He spoke throughout their history and into the time of and just beyond Jesus' life on our earth, always in the language and through the culture of his people. As one attempts to read and understand a passage of Scripture, one needs to be aware of its context, both historically and culturally.

SUMMARY

This chapter contains a number of hermeneutical tools of importance for determining the sacred author's intent in his formulating of Genesis 1 and 2 for its first recipients, the ancient people of Israel. Only after this step has been carried out can one rightfully apply these passages to the goal of this book, resolving the creation-evolution conflict.

First, the reader produces or obtains an accurate version of the biblical text, the content step, and the reader works from that. Then the context in which the passage was produced must be ascertained. In a crucial final step the reader attempts to understand the meaning of the text for its intended first recipients. The identification of the text's genre plays a crucial role in the understanding of its context. Biblical writers as well as Christian writers have legitimately used a number of nonliteral as well as literal genres in their writing. Jesus taught many times in the nonliteral form of parables. Jesus, biblical writers and modern Christian writers have found nonliteral genres such as parable, story, fantasy, myth and metaphor to be effective tools for telling truth in an understandable way.

A surprising and important step in understanding the nature of the Bible, particularly Genesis 1 and 2, is the recognition of the divine along with the incarnational character of the Bible. This parallels Jesus' character as both fully divine and fully human. The Bible's

---

[41]Ibid., p. 21.

incarnational nature is seen in the Genesis 1 and 2 creation narratives. They have the same form as the creation myths of ancient Israel's pagan neighbors but with an entirely different message as inspired by the Holy Spirit. Hence, applying passages such as Genesis 1 and 2 to a contemporary problem that was not a part of the life of the ancient Israelites requires a complex hermeneutical process.

An important step in our quest to resolve the creation-evolution conflict is to carefully study Genesis 1 and 2. But first we will study passages in the Bible other than Genesis 1 and 2, all passages in which creation plays a significant role. Here the intent is to apply the principle of comparing Scripture with Scripture. This will allow us to understand how creation was used in places in the Bible other than in Genesis. Then we will turn to Genesis 1 and 2.

4

Creation in the Old Testament

IN THIS CHAPTER, WE EXAMINE Old Testament creation passages, except for the first two chapters in Genesis. These include Isaiah 40, Job 38–41, some material from the proverbs and the creation psalms. The New Testament addresses creation more briefly in the prologue to the Gospel of John, in Romans and in the first chapters of the letters to the Colossians and the Hebrews, all to be discussed in chapter five. The biblical writers employ creation in these passages to address some rather important issues facing their original audiences. Recognizing this will aid in the understanding of the Genesis creation in chapter six, a detailed study of Genesis 1:1–2:3 and Genesis 2:4-25. The motivation for the biblical analysis is to aid in understanding the contribution biblical creation makes to the resolution of the conflict. This will move us closer to justifying the thesis of this book.

ISAIAH 40

In the 540s B.C., Isaiah 40 was written to comfort and encourage the Israelite exiles in Babylon through the prophet's announcement of their impending release from captivity (Is 40:1-11). In the remainder of the chapter (Is 40:12-31), the prophet argues persuasively that the LORD (God)[1] has the ability to bring about their release. He cites evi-

---

[1]In Is 40, God is referred to as the Hebrew Elohim (God) or YHWH (LORD). For sim-

dence from creation that the God of the universe, of creation and of the nations can and will bring this to reality. Isaiah 40–55, and in particular Isaiah 40, specifically spoke to the Israelite exiles in Babylon at that time.

Early in the sixth century, Jerusalem was destroyed at the hands of the Babylonians under Nebuchadnezzar. Most likely very few of the exiles addressed in Isaiah 40 remembered the horrific events of 597 and 587, as most of those who had been taken into exile were not still living by the 540s. Life in Babylonian captivity was not particularly cruel, but the exiles had little hope of returning to their homeland or of finding meaning in their remaining unhappy years in Babylon.[2] Even though the power of the neo-Babylonian empire was at its peak as it sacked Jerusalem in 587, by the middle of the sixth century this empire had begun to crumble. The Persians, under Cyrus, arose to become the Babylonians' chief threat. In 539 Cyrus arrived at the gates of Babylon and took the city without a battle.[3]

Isaiah took on the responsibility of ministering to the Israelite exiles in the late 540s. During their time of exile, the people of Israel, with the temple and the city of Jerusalem having been destroyed, were experiencing the deepest time of trouble and discouragement in their history. All of this was at the hands of a pagan people who ascribed their successes to their pagan gods, claiming they had defeated God. The people of Israel may have asked, has God annulled his covenant and abandoned us? Perhaps Marduk, the chief Babylonian god, killed God. The exiles needed a word of encouragement, a word of hope, a word reminding them who they were and a word regarding their destiny.[4]

Isaiah addressed the situation of the exiles. We can understand

---

plicity, the designation *God* will be frequently used throughout the discussion of Old Testament passages.

[2]George A. F. Knight, *Servant Theology: A Commentary on the Book of Isaiah 40—55,* International Theological Commentary (Grand Rapids: Eerdmans, 1984), pp. 13-14.

[3]R. N. Whybray, *The Second Isaiah* (Sheffield: JSOT Press, 1983), pp. 8-10.

[4]H. Darrell Lance, "Creation, Creationism, and Genesis 1," a paper presented to the Jamison Colloquium, University of Redlands, 1980 (unpublished).

Isaiah's strategy by examining the overall structure of Isaiah 40–55. There are two major divisions,[5] starting in chapters 40–48 with the theme of the announced liberation and action against Babylon. These chapters fall into the time period between 550 and 539 B.C. The second section, chapters 49–55, refers to the new community that would arise after the liberation, with this section dealing with events near 539 or slightly thereafter. Isaiah 40, the opening of the proclamation of liberation to the exiles, has two purposes. The first is to prophesy liberation to the captives, to call them to prepare to return to their homeland (Is 40:1-11). Later in Isaiah the prophet specifically names Cyrus of Persia as the liberator through whom God frees the exiles (Is 44:28; 45:1-3).

But the sacred prophet has a second purpose in this chapter. Given the discouraged state of mind of the exiles at that time and their questioning of God's existence, the prophet needs to convince the exiles that God is fully capable of bringing their announced liberation to reality. Isaiah faces an audience that is reluctant to believe his message of liberation. Consequently, he takes the role of an advocate for God, using a type of argumentation in sustaining the proclamation of liberation in Isaiah 40:1-11.[6] Isaiah needs to convince the exilic community that the Babylonian giant pales into insignificance in the meaningful structure of the universe, the structure ordered and sustained by God.[7]

Isaiah 40:12-31, a series of four disputation speeches, contains rhetorical questions designed to point out the ability of God to deliver the exiles from their captivity.[8] A disputation is a form of argument in which the speaker or writer, but not God, is a prophet. The literary

---

[5]Alberto Soggin, *Introduction to the Old Testament*, rev. ed. (Philadelphia: Westminster Press, 1980), p. 312.

[6]Whybray, *Second Isaiah*, p. 34.

[7]Klaus Koch, *The Prophets—The Babylonian and Persian Periods*, trans. Margaret Kohl (Philadelphia: Fortress, 1984), 2:134-35. (First German edition Stuttgart: Kohlhammer, 1978.)

[8]For example, see Koch, *Prophets*, 2:134; Whybray, *Second Isaiah*, p. 38; Knight, *Servant Theology*, pp. 18-26; John D. W. Watts, *Isaiah 34—66*, Word Biblical Commentary 25 (Waco, Tex.: Word, 1987), pp. 83-96.

form of the passage is poetic, and the style is interrogative. The four disputations are found in Isaiah 40:12-17, 18 + 21-24, 25-26 and 27-31. Verses 19-20 fall outside of the disputation structure.

First disputation: Isaiah 40:12-17. A series of ten rhetorical questions (verses 12-14) opens the first disputation. As the prophet addresses the exiles, he begins to develop the idea that God is the one and the only one with the capability to deliver the exiles from the power of Babylon and back to their homeland. The answers to the ten questions are obvious. The questions themselves and the related direct statements in the three verses to follow (verses 15-17) give important clues relating to God's ability and character.

In Isaiah 40:12-14, the question is raised in affirmation of God and in denial of Marduk, who but God has the creativity, power and knowledge to create the universe? In verse 12, who but God has the power to control and sustain creation? In verse 13, who teaches God, let alone really understands him? In verse 14, who advised God in creation? In these verses Isaiah asserts that only God is great enough and wise enough not only to plan and carry out creation but also to sustain the universe.

In Isaiah 40:15-17, the prophet turns to the nations of the earth. The assertion here is that the nations of the earth are as nothing when compared to God. Isaiah summarizes this line of reasoning in verse 17 by stating that all the nations together are a minus factor and less than nothing when measured against God.

After establishing the unique power of God compared to Marduk, Isaiah turns to address the immediate problem facing the exiles. Their problem centers on being woefully weak in comparison to almost any nearby nation, especially Babylon, but even to their announced liberators, the Persians. Here the prophet establishes a sense of metahistory; not only does God control creation, but he controls the political affairs of humankind.

Second disputation: Isaiah 40:18 + 21-24. The rhetorical question stated in verse 18, "To whom can you compare God?" explicitly brings out that which is implied in verses 13-14. The answer is obvious—no one, not even Marduk or any other Babylonian gods. This disputation then skips to verse 21, containing a follow-up to the question of verse 18. The reply comprises a series of four additional questions, designed to wake up the prophet's hearers, to bring them to attention and even to provoke them. (Teachers sometimes use the same kind of questions to say, "Can't you remember [fill in the blank]? As I recall we have already gone over this a number of times.") By these questions Isaiah asks the exiles to affirm God's activities in creation by responding positively to what he had just finished asserting in verses 12-17.

In Isaiah 40:22-24 the prophet reinforces what he has said about the nations in verses 15-17 but in somewhat different terms. In verse 22 he states that God rules supreme over the earth and heaven. Isaiah then points out in verse 23 that God judges the "great people" (political leaders?) of the earth, and these earthly powers cannot even briefly endure this judgment. In these verses Isaiah challenges the exiles to affirm that only God reigns supreme over all of the powers, over all of the "great people" of the earth, and hence over the Babylonians.

Once again Isaiah is dealing with the crucial issue of who, if anyone, controls history. The answer repeats the answer in verses 12-17, but in more explicit terms. It is God who exclusively created the universe and reigns as the lord of history.

Third disputation: Isaiah 40:25-26. The rhetorical question posed in verse 25 essentially repeats the questions raised in verse 18: is there any equal to God? If so, who? In this section the prophet emphasizes a point made in the first disputation, the comparison of God to Marduk implied in verses 13-14.

By directing the eyes of his hearers upward (this part of the speech must have been given at night as they looked at the stars) in Isaiah 40:26, Isaiah asks his audience to compare God to the astral deities of Babylon. Isaiah is pointing out that God, not Marduk or any of the other Babylonian gods, created everything in the heavens. Furthermore, YHWH knows each heavenly object by name and has so much control over and interest in the entire universe that not one heavenly object has ever been lost. Hence, God is both the creator of every object in the heavens and the one who maintains an individual relationship with each. Once again Isaiah is arguing that there is no comparison between God and any of the Babylonian gods.

Fourth disputation: Isaiah 40:27-31. A fundamental change occurs in the fourth disputation. The prophet no longer asks rhetorical questions; instead he responds directly to an actual complaint raised by the exilic community. The subject here, no longer the nature of God, centers on Israel's complaint of exile against God. It may be that addressing this complaint motivated the entire passage (Is 40:12-31). They ask, in effect, God, why don't you see our troubles? Why are our rights ignored by you? In other words, the exiles are claiming that God has neither been concerned nor fair with them.[9] But Isaiah turns their complaints around in verse 27 with the reply, how can you complain in this way?

In the last three verses (Is 40:29-31) the prophet completes this marvelously constructed chapter by reaching the goal referred to in the first word of the chapter, *comfort* (for the exiles). In verse 29 Isaiah asserts that it is God who gives comfort to those who are weak (the exilic community) by empowering and strengthening them out of his own resources. Isaiah reminds them (verse 30) that natural human strength, even at its best (in youths and the young) fails. But those weak and powerless who trust in God, those who have confidence in God's promise, will persevere and be supported with new strength and energy (verse 31). The NRSV depicts this as those who wait for the specific goal, God. Verses 30-31 develop two sides of a paradox. The strong will falter (verse 30). But the weak and powerless who trust (or wait) will complete the journey (verse 31).

The parenthetical passage: Isaiah 40:19-20. Verses 19 and 20 present the greatest exegetical challenge of the passage. One conclusion that has some merit suggests that verses 19 and 20 (even though there

---

[9]Watts, *Isaiah 34–66*, p. 96.

exists uncertainty about a number of details) consist of a sarcastic polemic against idolatry and thereby give support to the overall thought associated with the rhetorical questions. **Summary.** The central message of Isaiah 40:12-31 is that God has the ability to carry out his promises to his people. This passage focuses on God and his relation to creation, to history, to pagan "deities" and to his people.

R. N. Whybray concludes that Isaiah was addressing basic Israelite beliefs in God through his creation references in Isaiah 40:12-31. God reminds the exiles, point by point, that their theological traditions about creation are more credible than those of the Babylonians.[10] H. Darrell Lance argues that the creation narrative of Genesis 1 played the same role for the exilic community[11] as Whybray concludes in reference to Isaiah 40. Frederic Bush points out that the creation narratives of Genesis may have been first inscripturated during the exile or shortly thereafter, perhaps by Ezra,[12] although the time of final formulation of any parts of the Pentateuch remains in question. Thorleif Bowman[13] suggests that the idea of God creating is a conclusion rather than an axiom of the Old Testament. He also asserts that creation starts as a gospel in Isaiah and ends as doctrine (as religious philosophy and history) in Genesis 1, and that the basic ideas about creation are the same in both books. He concludes that in Isaiah and throughout Scripture the ideas of creation and salvation are synonymous.

To summarize, Isaiah addressed the greatest difficulty faced up to that time by the people of Israel, that of the Babylonian exile. He did this through posing and then answering a series of rhetorical questions by appealing to YHWH as the creator, controller, sustainer and wisdom of all creation.

---

[10]Whybray, *Second Isaiah,* pp. 54-57.

[11]Lance, "Creation, Creationism, and Genesis 1."

[12]Frederic Wm. Bush, "The Historical Nature of the Primeval Tradition," in *Supplement to Old Testament Survey and Selected Readings,* pp. 23-34 (unpublished).

[13]Thorleif Bowman, "The Biblical Doctrine of Creation," *Church Quarterly Review* 165 (1964): 140.

WISDOM IN THE OLD TESTAMENT

Old Testament wisdom[14] is generally regarded to consist of the wisdom psalms along with the books of Proverbs, Ecclesiastes and Job. In wisdom writing, an emphasis exists not on God as the redeemer or as the God of the exodus, but rather on the creator God who undergirds the human race and every society.

Wisdom writing focuses on the individual. Questions are addressed, such as how does an individual relate to life? How does an individual obey God? How does an individual deal with personal crises? Wisdom, from the theological point of view, is concerned with the divine order of the created world based on the framework of a theology of creation.

In wisdom writings, God can set aside his rules by breaking the rules or allowing the rules to be broken in certain situations. Sometimes life is really not all that orderly in the way that we would prefer it to be. Exceptions to the rules include such things as disaster in the life of a good person. Sometimes life simply doesn't seem to be fair. As a result, there are levels of wisdom displayed in the Old Testament.

Proverbs contains what could be called basic or conventional wisdom. The principle here is that wisdom leads to life and folly to death, with righteousness being rewarded while sin is punished. In gaining wisdom, a person can live life beneficially to both that person and those this person encounters. Proverbs, a thoroughly theological book, asks the reader to ponder some basic questions, such as what should be the driving force of my life? Will I enter into a relationship with Wisdom or Folly? with God or idols? Proverbs provides a basic education in wisdom, and in terms of a college curriculum, the course of Proverbs is Wisdom 101—Introduction to Principles of Wisdom.

Ecclesiastes and Job present more sophisticated wisdom.[15] Ec-

---

[14]William Sanford LaSor, David Allan Hubbard and Frederic Wm. Bush, *Old Testament Survey: The Message, Form, and Background of the Old Testament* (Grand Rapids: Eerdmans, 1982), pp. 542-46.

[15]Tremper Longman III, *Reading the Bible with Heart and Mind* (Colorado Springs: NavPress, 1997), pp. 88-89.

clesiastes, using the voice of the Teacher, does not question the wisdom of Proverbs but comes to the further conclusion that life is meaningless. And yet at the end of the book the Teacher advises that the best course in life is to "fear God and obey his commands" (Eccles 12:13). The Ecclesiastes college course is Wisdom 201—Advanced Topics in Wisdom.

The book of Job[16] confronts the thought of Proverbs in a different way, for in the system of Proverbs a person like Job cannot be found. According to Proverbs, if Job were truly righteous, he would find life, wealth and health. But the book of Job shows wisdom, as in Ecclesiastes, to be a bit more complex. A dominant theme in Proverbs is that, generally speaking, good and wise conduct is rewarded. But, this is not the entire story in Job or in Proverbs, for Proverbs states that it is possible to be wise and at the same time poor, and the better choice is wisdom when a choice must be made. In Job we find a righteous person who is a grievous sufferer. At the same time, the book of Job shows that a truly religious attitude is not always passive resignation to misfortune but may include the courage to enter into dispute with God. The book of Job introduces surprise and paradox into the understanding of how our world operates. This course is Wisdom 501—a graduate school Ph.D. seminar on wisdom.

In this section, creation will be considered as it is used in Proverbs, and then as it plays the key role in a longer passage in Job.

Basic wisdom—Proverbs 3:19-20 and 8:22-31. In Proverbs 3:19-20 the writer links wisdom, understanding and knowledge, not to distinguish them but to show that understanding and knowledge are facets of wisdom.[17] The ultimate reason for taking wisdom seriously, according to the writer, is that God did so when creating the cosmos.[18]

The Proverbs 8 passage contains a speech by Wisdom that needs

---

[16]Ibid.

[17]David A. Hubbard, *Proverbs,* Communicator's Commentary Series (Waco, Tex.: Word Books, 1989), p. 75.

[18]John Goldingay, "Proverbs," in *New Bible Commentary,* ed. G. J. Wenham, J. A. Motyer, D. A. Carson and R. T. France (Downers Grove, Ill.: InterVarsity Press, 1994), p. 589.

to be read figuratively and not literally.[19] Wisdom is to be seen as a personification of God's wisdom. As such, this passage describes Wisdom's presence and role in creation, because she is formed by God before anything else is created. Thus Wisdom has existed from before the beginning, and this passage makes the point that God creates the universe by his already-existing Wisdom. We find here that God uses Wisdom—mind, intelligence and common sense—in planning and carrying out creation. Hence, Wisdom not only witnesses creation but also participates in it. We find good reason for placing Wisdom over all the other virtues.[20] This passage has many parallels with creation in Genesis 1. Examples include the oceans referred to in Genesis 1:2 and Proverbs 8:24 and pushing back the waters in Genesis 1:9-13 and Proverbs 8:29. The goodness and orderliness of creation are also seen throughout Genesis 1 and Proverbs 8:22-31.[21]

Advanced wisdom—Job 38–41. Job 38–41 is another example in which creation plays a key role in addressing a serious problem, the theme of the suffering. Additionally, Job evaluates conventional wisdom. The book considers a number of questions. Do innocent people suffer, or is suffering always deserved? Expressed in another way, is all human suffering a result of divine judgment on sinfulness?[22] The second question—what are the origins of suffering?—does not receive a satisfactory answer in Job. This question is indeed raised and discussed but never really resolved. Even after the voice of God comes to Job in the whirlwind (Job 38–39; 40:6–41:34), does Job really get an answer? David Clines concludes that the book of Job does not regard the origins of suffering as the primary question.[23]

The first question receives a clear answer, that suffering is not al-

---

[19]Tremper Longman III, *Proverbs* (Grand Rapids: Baker Academic, 2006), pp. 104-5.

[20]Hubbard, *Proverbs*, pp. 123-26; Goldingay, "Proverbs," pp. 591-92.

[21]Longman, *Proverbs,* pp. 104-5.

[22]J. Gerald Janzen, "On the Moral Nature of God's Power: Yahweh and the Sea in Job and Deutero-Isaiah," *Catholic Biblical Quarterly* 56 (July 1994): 458-78.

[23]David J. A. Clines, "Job," in *New Bible Commentary,* ed. D. A. Carson, R. T. France, J. A. Motyer and G. J. Wenham (Downers Grove, Ill.: InterVarsity Press, 1994), pp. 459-61.

ways what should happen to a person (see Job 1:1; 6:30; 9:15; and God's response in 42:7, 8). The truth of this raises a problem, for if the prospect exists that an innocent person can suffer, then logically only two possibilities seem to follow. Either God is just but not omnipotent, or God is omnipotent but not just. In the book of Job these issues are explored through the voice in the whirlwind as it points out a number of aspects of creation.[24] But this too is not the primary point about suffering made in this book.

According to Clines, the third and most important question is a more personal question, how can I suffer? What am I to do when suffering? Clines declares that the entire book of Job is required to answer this question.[25] Two answers are given. The first is found early in the book. After Job experiences various grievous calamities (Job 1:6-19 and 2:4-7), he blesses God for what God gives and what God takes away (Job 1:21), both for good and for harm (Job 2:10). Here Job calmly accepts what appears to be God's will. But this calm acceptance lasts only for the first two chapters. Then Job's three friends, Eliphaz, Bildad and Zophar, come on the scene to join and advise Job as he suffers. The second answer to this question results from Job's turmoil and distress (Job 3–31), as he can no longer accept what has happened to him. This section of the book contains a series of speeches by Job and responses by his three friends, responses with a variety of commentary and advice directed toward Job. These are mostly inappropriate and unhelpful. After enduring their words for some time, Job becomes bitter and angry, and he even feels persecuted by God. At this point Job no longer suppresses his hostility for his situation but instead complains and shouts his anger and frustration directly toward God. Clines writes that Job at times is rash and unjust in the way he speaks of God, and yet Job's protests are spoken in the right direction. Job needs to encounter God.[26]

And because Job continues to address (scream at) God, God re-

[24]Janzen, "On the Moral Nature," pp. 458-78.
[25]Clines, "Job," p. 459.
[26]Ibid.

sponds by his two speeches to Job out of the whirlwind in Job 38–41. The two speeches bring some closure to the agony Job is experiencing as he tries to understand his situation. What may be most surprising is that God actually responds to Job's cries by means of these speeches. And so God meets Job in his distress. However, as Clines points out,[27] (1) Job's suffering does not end even though God responds to him; (2) Job discovers he has misjudged God; (3) at the same time Job finds his anguish somehow calmed because of his encounter with God; and (4) despite Job's bitter words against God, God meets Job in an amazing response and praises him for speaking "accurately about me [the LORD]" (Job 42:8).

Clines writes,

> What the friends say about suffering in general may well be true in other circumstances. But where they fail Job is that they take their cue from their doctrine instead of from the evidence of their eyes and ears. They know that Job is a good man, and they wrong him by thinking that his suffering is a witness against his goodness. The book of Job is not against the friends, but it wants to say that suffering happens to good people who do not deserve it as well as to people who deserve all that happens to them.[28]

Analysis of Job 38–41. In Job 31, Job answers the accusations by his friends in a speech in which he declares his innocence and strongly requests (demands) that God produce a list of charges against him (Job 31:35-37). Chapters 38–41 contain an amazing pair of speeches out of the whirlwind by which God directly answers Job. These chapters address the major problem of the book as God actually meets Job face to face in response to his cry of distress. An important feature of God's response comes in a recitation of some fundamental features of creation. And ultimately this brings relief in an unexpected way to Job. The essence of God's (the LORD's) speeches in chapters 38–41 is sur-

---

[27]Ibid., p. 460.
[28]Ibid.

prise and paradox, all couched in terms of characteristics of creation and the created order. Hence, God does not speak directly to the question of Job's suffering. In referring to the cosmic order and the animal creation, God does not simply give Job some scientific information. Instead, God asks Job to consider the mystery and complexity of the created order that God himself fashioned, and to learn important principles from that. The point is that the natural order of the universe parallels the moral order in many ways, some of the natural order being beyond human understanding. Some aspects seem hideous, futile, wasteful or fearsome, but all represent the work of a wise God who intentionally made the cosmos in the way it is for his own purposes.[29]

Job 38:1–40:2—The LORD (God) speaks: Consider the mystery of creation. Focusing entirely on his creation in the first speech, the voice in the whirlwind points out ten physical features of the created order (Job 38:4-38) and then refers to nine species of animals. As examples of physical features of creation, God includes such things as his decision on the size of the earth (one of the important physical parameters of our earth-sun system); the mechanism of how the oceans are kept separate from the lands; the mechanism that produces the earth's diurnal cycle of day and night; the source of light; and how rain, snow and ice are produced. God speaks to Job asking, who is responsible for all of these features? Can you, God inquires, control them? Do you have the wisdom to plan them? Do you understand them? Or is all of this a mystery to you?

Next, God points out nine somewhat strange species of animals (Job 38:39–39:30) to illustrate the mystery of created life. All manner of animals are mentioned, the lion, wild goat, deer, wild donkey, wild ox, ostrich, horse, hawk and eagle. Some of these are useful to humans, some a threat, some seemingly useless, some apparently rather stupid, some filled with wisdom, some fierce and some mysterious, but God cites all as examples of his created order, a creation under his plan, power and care.

---

[29]Ibid., p. 481.

Do these chapters have a parallel with suffering? Is it sometimes that suffering may have a recognizable purpose, but other times suffering is just as enigmatic, mysterious and even hurtful to humans as certain wild animals can be, animals who are part of the created order? God points out to Job that all features of the cosmos and all animals are the result of his creation, all part of his deliberate order for the universe. If Job understands this, then can Job also accept the fact that at least some cases of human suffering arise simply from the unfathomable wisdom of God in terms of the overall plan of creation, a wisdom beyond human understanding?[30]

At the conclusion of this speech (Job 40:1-2) the LORD does not criticize Job. He simply asks Job if he wants to go on with the discussion, saying in essence that since Job had initiated the encounter, he can respond if he wishes.

Job 40:3-5—Job's response to the first speech. "I am nothing—how could I ever find the answers. . . . I have said too much already. I have nothing more to say" (Job 40:4a, 5). In effect, Job simply asks God to continue his speech. But Job does not express submission, humiliation or defeat.

Job 40:6–41:34—The LORD speaks: Consider the power of creation. The main point of the introductory paragraph (Job 40:6-14) of the second speech is God's justice, not his power, and the vindication of a person. Job is demanding vindication. However, only one with power like that of God's ("Are you as strong as God?" [Job 40:9]) and in physical control of the universe can have the authority to make judgments in the moral sphere also.[31] In response, Job gives no indication of a willingness to take on the divine role of managing the cosmos.

The creation theme of the previous chapter continues by the presentation of two loving descriptions of the Behemoth, the fiercest of the land animals (perhaps a hippopotamus, a wild buffalo or a mythological creature), and the Leviathan (possibly a crocodile or another mythological animal), the most dreadful of the sea creatures. These

---

[30]Ibid., pp. 481-82.
[31]Ibid., p. 483.

animals, symbols of chaos, were created by God, who at all times controls their chaotic powers that could threaten the universe. Is God's point here that suffering is like a Behemoth, like a Leviathan, terrifying, mysterious and powerful, yet a deliberate part of creation with its own splendor, and ultimately created by and under God's direction and control?

Job 42:1-6—Job responds: Worship replaces his demands and criticism. At the conclusion of God's second speech, Job is ready to reply. But now he recognizes his inadequacy to deal with the questions he raised. Job realizes that he lacks wisdom and lacks God's attributes. Almost by default Job's anger and questioning of God come to an end. Job recognizes God's right to create and govern the universe as he chooses, even to the extent of allowing an innocent person to suffer. Even though Job does not actually say this in so many words, it is clear that Job's anger, frustration and anxiety have come to an end, for Job worships and repents. Job affirms the goodness and wisdom of not only creation but also how the universe is governed by God. He recognizes that his own wisdom counts as ignorance next to God's wisdom and that meeting God face to face is far better that having the answers he is seeking. Job addresses God as follows, "I know that you can do anything, and no one can stop you. You asked, 'Who is this that questions my wisdom with such ignorance?' It is I—and I was talking about things I knew nothing about, things far too wonderful for me" (Job 42:2-3).

Clines points out that in Job 42:2, Job is saying not that God is omnipotent but rather that God has an inescapable purpose in whatever he does. Job declares that his suffering makes sense to God, even though God did not explain or justify it to him. Job has realized that he was mistaken to demand an answer to the reason for his suffering, for this would be to intrude into an area beyond human comprehension.[32] For Job the most significant aspect of his encounter with God is that he met God face to face.

---

[32]Ibid.

Conclusion. Isaiah employed creation as his most powerful argument in encouraging the exiles to end the most difficult situation the people of Israel had ever faced to that time. In much the same way, the writer of the book of Job used the voice of God out of the whirlwind, again referring exclusively to creation, to resolve Job's crisis of faith. The suffering of an innocent person may well be the deepest of personal crises that one can experience. In considering Isaiah 40 and Job 38–41, a picture begins to develop of the type of circumstances in which the sacred authors of the Old Testament chose creation by which to address a particular issue.

PSALMS OF CREATION

Understanding the psalms requires a knowledge of how they were used in the life of Israel.[33] Evidence exists showing that the vast majority of the psalms were utilized within the context of worship in the temple and the synagogue. The psalms were sung in worship, making their poetic form appropriate.

Creation plays a prominent role in a number of the psalms. As Walter Brueggemann points out,[34] a foundational prerequisite for a sense of well-being results from the experience of the regularity of life, including nature's regularities as articulated in the hymn "Great Is Thy Faithfulness." And a number of the creation psalms echo the thought of Genesis 1.

Psalm 8. Each aspect of creation in Psalm 8[35] relates to features found in the Genesis 1 creation account and, as such, lies within the mainstream of biblical creation. Just as in Genesis 1, there is order in Psalm 8, and Psalm 8 affirms God as the creator of what is in the heavens as well as the inhabitants of the earth. Psalm 8:4-8 affirms and celebrates

---

[33]Nicolaas Herman Ridderbos and Peter C. Craigie, "Psalms," in *The International Standard Bible Encyclopedia,* ed. Geoffrey W. Bromiley, Everett F. Harrison, Roland K. Harrison, William Sanford LaSor, Lawrence T. Geraty and Edgar W. Smith Jr. (Grand Rapids: Eerdmans, 1986), 3:1033.
[34]Walter Brueggemann, *The Message of the Psalms—A Theological Commentary* (Minneapolis: Augsburg, 1984), pp. 28-38.
[35]Ibid., pp. 36-38.

the high position of humankind in the created order. This is in harmony with God's creative actions and the declaration of humanity's governorship over the created order as found on the sixth day in Genesis 1.

Psalm 19. Psalm 19,[36] classified as a creation psalm, contains two distinct parts. In the creation hymn (Ps 19:1-6) the psalmist points out the extraterrestrial witness of the heavens, the skies, day and night, and the sun, all testimony to the glory of God in ways inaudible to human ears. The second part (Ps 19:7-14) consists of a meditation on God's written word that reveals his will in verses 7-10, to which the worshiper responds in verses 11-14.

Romans 1:18-20 clearly reflects the thought of Psalm 19:1-6 as Paul points out that "through everything God made, they [people] can clearly see his invisible qualities—his eternal power and divine nature" (Rom 1:20).

In both passages the witness of creation to God's "glory" (Ps 19) and God's "invisible qualities" (Rom 1) are examples of what would be called "wordless speech," a kind of speech that is "heard" by all throughout the world.

Psalm 19:4-6 expresses a deep human response to the wonder of being and the majestic order of the cosmos, conveying faith in God not simply as a power of nature but as the Creator transcending the cosmos.

The psalmist does not say that the heavens reveal God. Instead, the celestial phenomena specifically make known God's glory and give praise to the Creator by functioning as they do. However, these do not disclose who God is or God's purpose. Psalm 19 and Romans 1 declare the existence of a kind of knowledge available to humanity through contemplating the works of creation, but this knowledge does not refer to a saving knowledge through Jesus Christ. These passages provide a starting point for what would be called a theology of nature.

---

[36]Bernhard W. Anderson, *Out of the Depths—The Psalms Speak for Us Today* (Philadelphia: Westminster Press, 1983), pp. 145-48; Derek Kidner, *Psalms 1-72—An Introduction and Commentary,* Tyndale Old Testament Commentaries (Downers Grove, Ill.: InterVarsity Press, 1973), pp. 97-100.

Psalm 33. The first two lines of each eight-line stanza (Ps 33:4-7, 8-11) present the LORD (YHWH) as Creator through his creative word. Verse 4 tells of his word and work that are inseparable and verse 5 of his unfailing love, all of which are the reasons for the outburst of praise in the preceding verses. Just as in Genesis 1, the psalmist here (Ps 33:6, 9) tells of creation by God's spoken and powerful word. The LORD speaks, and as a result the heavens are created; the LORD breathes the word, and the stars are born. And in verse 9 the LORD speaks and the world begins to appear at his command. These are echoes of creation found in Genesis 1, the main difference being that God (Elohim) speaks creation into existence in Genesis 1, whereas here in Psalm 33 it is the LORD speaking creation into existence. This difference, not substantive, simply reflects differences in style of the writers in their designations for God. Psalm 33 intimates the idea of *creatio ex nihilo* (i.e., creation from nothing) in which a totally free God creates the world apart from any forces external to his loving desire to bring such a world into existence,[37] a concept also encountered in Genesis 1. In Psalm 33:6 the LORD "merely spoke, and the heavens were created." And in verse 9, "when he spoke, the world began! It appeared at his command."

Next a statement of God's power over people and nations is expressed by the psalmist in the form of a number of verbs describing God's characteristic actions. These include "frustrates the plans," "thwarts," "stand firm," "can never be shaken," "looks down," "sees," "observes," "made" and "understands." God's power and actions result in the experience of joy for the nation whose God is the LORD (Ps 33:12), whereas human plans are futile given God's overriding sovereignty (Ps 33:16-17). The confidence expressed by the psalmist here recalls the tone of Isaiah 40:12-17; in that passage the prophet also gives witness to God's creative activity and governing power over the nations.[38]

---

[37]Ted Peters, "Editor's Introduction—Pannenberg on Theology and Natural Science," in Wolfhart Pannenberg, *Toward a Theology of Nature: Essays on Science and Faith,* ed. Ted Peters (Louisville, Ky.: Westminster John Knox, 1993), p. 11.

[38]Brueggemann, *Message of the Psalms,* pp. 34-35.

The climactic five verses begin with Psalm 33:18, a reminder of the latter verses of Isaiah 40. The psalmist, noting the awesome creative power of God and applying it to the present needs of his people, declares that God watches over and rescues those who fear him. **Psalm 74.** Psalm 74,[39] a communal lament, mourns the destruction of the temple and Jerusalem that marked the beginning of the Babylonian exile. Lament characterizes the psalm's beginning and end. But suddenly and surprisingly, a burst of praise appears in the middle of this psalm in verses 12-17. This praise centers on creation, on God as king, savior, conqueror and creator. This section is dominated by the pronoun *you*, referring to God, his past actions and perhaps even what is expected of him at that time. The first *you* recalls God's power over various opposing entities, and the last *you* affirms God as the lord of creation. The psalmist concludes this lament by praying for God to bring this horrible situation to a just and right end.

Psalm 104. Psalm 104, an exquisite descriptive hymn of Israel's creation faith, can be called a creation rhapsody and an extended celebration of the goodness, magnificent character and splendor of creation. This psalm can also be considered a commentary on Genesis 1[40] and the celebration of the order, symmetry and majesty of creation found in Isaiah 40:12-17 and Job 38–41.[41] For example, the parallels Bernard Anderson finds between this psalm and Genesis 1 are as follows:[42]

- Psalm 104:2-4, cf. Genesis 1:6-8—God stretches out the curtain of the heavens

- Psalm 104:5-9, cf. Genesis 1:9-10—God establishes bounds for the waters

[39]Leslie C. Allen, *Psalms*, Word Biblical Themes (Waco, Tex.: Word, 1987), pp. 19, 37; Brueggemann, *Message of the Psalms*, pp. 68-71.

[40]J. A. Motyer, "Psalms," in *New Bible Commentary*, ed. D. A. Carson, R. T. France, J. A. Motyer and G. J. Wenham (Downers Grove, Ill.: InterVarsity Press, 1994), pp. 553-54; Anderson, *Out of the Depths*, pp. 156-60.

[41]Brueggemann, *Message of the Psalms*, p. 32.

[42]Anderson, *Out of the Depths*, p. 158.

- Psalm 104:10-13, cf. Genesis 1:6-10—God causes springs and rain to bring water

- Psalm 104:14-18, cf. Genesis 1:11-12—God provides vegetation and food for birds, animals and humans

- Psalm 104:19-23, cf. Genesis 1:14-18—God creates the moon and the sun, resulting in day and night

- Psalm 104:24-26, cf. Genesis 1:20-22—God creates the seas and life in the sea

- Psalm 104:27-30, cf. Genesis 1:24-30—The dependence of animals and humans on God for their creation and life

Psalm 104, just as in Genesis 1, exhibits a picture of the order and design of a marvelous creation. The affirming judgment by God of the entire creation in Genesis 1:31 is echoed in this psalm as it comes to an end in verses 31-35.

Psalm 145. Psalm 145, another psalm of creation, praises the LORD, not for anything spectacular but for the daily occurrence of life's regularities experienced as reliable, equitable and generous. This characteristic of creation can be understood as one way of God's bestowing blessing on us. And because of this, the psalmist expresses Israel's joyous and grateful confidence in God. The truth proclaimed throughout the psalm, that God governs the world in a way that can be counted on, makes modern science possible. As Brueggemann ends his commentary on this psalm, he writes, "We take Psalm 145 to be the fullest representative of those psalms that understand creation as a mode of equilibrium, coherence, and reliability. Such a presentation of life is an act of high faith."[43]

Psalm 148. This psalm has been called "creation praise," "choir of creation" and "hymn to God the creator." The entire created order is summoned to praise the LORD. These worshiping elements include angels; cosmic and earthly objects such as the sun, moon, skies and vapors; the land and sea animals; elements of weather; mountains

---

[43]Brueggemann, *Message of the Psalms*, p. 31.

and hills; trees; and all people from kings to children to old men. All are to give praise to the name of the LORD.[44]

Summary. For the most part, the creation psalms were used in the worship of the ancient people of Israel and are joyous songs of praise to God for his creative power, care and wisdom. Notable is the consistency of themes in creation passages throughout the Old Testament. Echoes of Genesis 1, Isaiah 40 and Job 38–41 are found in many of the creation psalms.

---

[44]Ibid., p. 165.

5

Creation in the New Testament

JOHN—THE PROLOGUE

The Gospel of John,[1] an amazing piece of literature, differs from all else in the Bible. Like the other three (Synoptic) Gospels, the Gospel of John centers on Jesus. Each of the four Gospels presents a unique portrait of Jesus. But whereas the Synoptics are primarily historical accounts starting with Jesus' infancy, the Gospel of John starts at *the* beginning, the beginning of all before creation. Instead of a historical account, John's Gospel functions as more of a theological commentary on Jesus, designed to fulfill the purpose stated near the very end of the Gospel: "But these are written so that you may continue to believe that Jesus is the Messiah, the Son of God, and that by believing in him you will have life by the power of his name" (Jn 20:31).

The Gospel of John[2] does not begin with the historical incarnate Jesus; instead, we are introduced to the Word (Greek: *logos*), who is not identified as Jesus Christ until the end of the prologue.

John 1:1-5—The preexistent Word. The opening words of John's Gospel remind one of those of Genesis 1, with the addition here that

[1]Donald Guthrie, "John," in *New Bible Commentary,* ed. G. J. Wenham, J. A. Motyer, D. A. Carson and R. T. France (Downers Grove, Ill.: InterVarsity Press, 1994), pp. 1021-23.

[2]Ibid., pp. 1024-27; William Hendriksen, *New Testament Commentary—Exposition of the Gospel According to John* (Grand Rapids: Baker, 1953), pp. 69-91.

the Word existed before creation. The three verbs in John 1:1 are all third-person singular imperfect active indicative, implying past but continuing action. And so the Word that now is, was in existence before the initiation of creation. This introduces a profound theme, one that is enhanced by the next two statements. The first phrase could be translated, "and the Word was face to face with God." The preposition *pros*, translated as "with," implies more than this single word. The full meaning is in the sense of "in communion with" or "in the presence of." This, followed by the second phrase, declares that the Word is God, is deity.

John then proclaims the creative activity of the Word. The Word was not created, for the Word was and is. All things, one by one, were created through the Word. The possibility of creation apart from the Word is excluded here. The key role of the Word in creation, consistent with what will be subsequently observed in Colossians 1 and Hebrews 1, proclaims the second person of the Trinity as the agent of the Godhead who carried out creation.

The sacred writer then turns to the subjects of light and darkness. The connection is made between light and life. Just as in the physical world life depends on light, so in the spiritual world does life depend on light. This light, closely related to the Word, tells us that the spiritual light that humankind has received is a result of the coming of the Word. Furthermore, active resistance to the light does not destroy it. Throughout Scripture, beginning with its creation in Genesis 1:3, light plays an important and positive role, having been created by God on creation's first day, and is used as a metaphor in verses such as Psalms 36:9 and 104:2. Light is always associated with the godly or good attributes of people.

John 1:6-8—The witness of John the Baptist. In these three verses, a comparison is made between John the Baptist (Jn 1:6-8) and the Word (Jn 1:1, 2, 9). See the comparison in table 1.

John 1:9-13—The light coming into the world. He who is coming into the world is identified by John as the "true light, who gives light to everyone." Consistent with this declaration, in John 8:12 Jesus

Table 1. Comparison of Christ the Word and John the Baptist in John 1:6-8

The Word	John the Baptist
Christ the Word	John
Preexistent	Was sent
Is the Word	Is a man
Is God	Commissioned by God
The light	Not the light, but a witness to the light

himself declares, "I am the light of the world. If you follow me, you won't have to walk in darkness, because you will have the light that leads to life." Jesus' rejection by some is foretold by John, along with the invitation for those who believe him and accept him to become children of God, a nonphysical rebirth from God.

John 1:14-18—The incarnation of the Word. The latter part of the prologue is an account of the Word becoming human, the incarnation. There is absolute certainty that the identification of the incarnate (human) Jesus, who walked among real people at a certain place and at a certain time, talked with people, ate and drank with people, and died just like any other person who has lived, is indeed the preexistent Word, is God, is the second person of the Trinity, and is God's agent of creation.

PAUL'S DISCUSSION OF THE CREATION

Romans 1:18-20. The apostle Paul wrote to the Christian church in Rome. A number of Paul's epistles are letters to a particular church with which he had already established a relationship, the purpose of many letters was to address specific questions or problems that had arisen in that church. But in the letter to the Romans, Paul focuses on some general and important theological principles not only for the Romans but also for believers throughout the world. In fact, the first twelve chapters of the letter could be called, The Gospel According to Paul.

Romans 1:1-17 contains an introductory statement, greetings, ex-

planations and a summary of the theme of the letter, the righteousness of God revealed. Paul then addresses the first theological theme
of the letter, the gospel and the righteousness of God by faith (Rom
1:18–4:25[3] and 5:21[4]), or as F. F. Bruce put it, "sin and retribution: the
universal need diagnosed (Rom 1:18–3:20)" and "the way of righteousness: the universal need met (Rom 3:21–5:21)."[5]

A passage relevant to the discussion of creation is the first three
verses of this theological discourse as it begins in Romans 1:18. Paul
begins to make the case for humanity's universal need for redemption by pointing out the widespread condition of paganism. Paul
asks, how did this paganism arise? He replies that its origin is in
wrong conceptions of God. These wrong ideas did not arise inno-
cently, but as he points out in Romans 1:19 and 20, true knowledge of
God is accessible to everyone.

This is the key idea. Paul is saying that, as each person observes
earth, sky and everything God has made, two important qualities of
God are clearly seen, his eternal power and his divine nature. Theo-
logically this is called general revelation, and from this alone a natural
theology can begin to be formed. According to Paul, this is a sufficient
start toward theism, but it does not directly result in a Christology or
Christianity. However, this can result in a movement from atheism
and agnosticism toward theism and the recognition of God's existence. Furthermore, evidence of this sort is available to all.

Romans 8:19-23. In Romans 8 Paul continues his theological discourse begun in Romans 1, focusing on the eschaton and, in the five
verses of interest here, commenting on redemption. It may be surprising that here Paul suggests that redemption includes the entire
created order, a redemption of both humanity and all things nonhu-

---

[3]Douglas J. Moo, "Romans," in *New Bible Commentary*, ed. G. J. Wenham, J. A. Motyer,
D. A. Carson and R. T. France (Downers Grove, Ill.: InterVarsity Press, 1994), pp.
1115-22.
[4]James D. G. Dunn, *Romans 1-8*, Word Biblical Commentary 38A (Dallas: Word,
1988), pp. 50-59.
[5]F. F. Bruce, *Romans*, Tyndale New Testament Commentaries (Leicester, U.K.: Inter-
Varsity Press, 1985), pp. 77, 94.

man (Rom 8:19). Recall the beginning of John 3:16, "For God loved the world so much that he gave his one and only Son." The Greek word translated as "world" is *cosmos,* and hence Jesus reveals God's love for the entire cosmos. Redemption is cosmic. Addressing the nonhuman creation specifically in Romans 8:20-22, the apostle points out that all creation is under God's curse, referring to the curse in Genesis 3 resulting from humanity's sin. Creation is subject to death and decay, groaning as in the pains of childbirth. But Paul declares that there will be a future day in which creation will join God's children in freedom from this death and decay, and that creation will be restored to the original very good condition (Gen 1:31) in order to fulfill God's original intent for it.

Paul is not declaring an annihilation of the created order but rather a transformation, perhaps a cosmos that will be described by new laws of physics. Did Jesus, in his post-resurrection body as he spent some time on earth before his ascension, experience these new laws of physics? During those days on earth Jesus did not seem to have been moving about in a way that would be understood in terms of our laws of physics, as can be implied from Luke 24:13-37 and John 20:11-29. The redemption of all creation implies that the universe will not experience any of the bad endings as predicted by cosmologists.

Colossians 1:15-20—The cosmic Christ. In his letter to the Colossian church, the apostle Paul expresses his understanding of some cosmic aspects of the basic character of Jesus Christ in the hymn found in Colossians 1:15-20. There are five characteristics or roles of Jesus in this hymn that merit attention.

Jesus' role in the creation of the universe. By far the majority of biblical references to creation are found in the Old Testament. In all Old Testament creation passages the creator is God, referred to as YHWH (God) or YHWH Elohim (LORD God), and is the monotheistic Hebrew God. Even though there may be slight hints of a trinitarian concept of God in the Old Testament, it is not until the New Testament that the clear identification of the agent in the trinitarian Godhead responsible for creation is the second person of the Trinity, the

Word who became flesh, Christ Jesus. This is clearly stated in this passage from Colossians and in the prologue to the Gospel of John, and again will be seen in the prologue to the letter to the Hebrews.

Jesus' role in the ongoing operation of the universe. There is more besides creation. Both the Colossians and Hebrews passages declare that Jesus is the one who upholds the universe: "and he [Christ] holds all creation together" (Col 1:17); "and he [the Son] sustains everything by the mighty power of his command" (Heb 1:3).

Jesus, now with his resurrection power and glory, keeps the entire universe running in what we observe to be a consistent and faithful way. What scientists discover through their investigations and their empirical determinations of the laws of nature are simply a reflection of how Jesus so faithfully and powerfully sustains all things. All things hold together and consistently behave in terms of these scientific descriptions because of Jesus' faithfulness in this role. The corollary to this is if Jesus withdrew his sustaining providential care, the universe would then instantly collapse into nothingness. As a result, everything observed about our universe, our earth, nature itself and how our bodies function reflects the consistent upholding and sustaining, caring love and power of Jesus.

Jesus' basic character and the principle of complementarity. Recall the following paradoxical verses:

Christ is the visible image of the invisible God. (Col 1:15)

For God in all his fullness was pleased to live in Christ. (Col 1:19)

In the beginning the Word already existed. The Word was with God, and the Word was God. (Jn 1:1)

The Son radiates God's own glory and expresses the very character of God. (Heb 1:3)

So the Word became human and made his home among us. (Jn 1:14)

The early church struggled to find a category by which to classify Jesus. Here was this person who had walked among them, enjoyed a party eating and drinking with his friends, doing the things people do. But there was more, as Jesus healed and taught like no one ever had. A voice from heaven had declared, "You are my dearly loved Son" (Mk 1:11) and "This is my Son, my Chosen One" (Lk 9:35). And no other has ever died and then been resurrected back to life. So, who is this person? How is Jesus to be understood? Into what category do we classify him? The early church came to a solution at the Council of Chalcedon in 451, with the rather simple but startling declaration that Jesus is both fully human and fully God. This brings to mind the wave-particle duality and the principle of complementarity in quantum physics; these deal with the evidence, gathered at the microscopic level, that all entities in the universe possess both wavelike and particlelike properties. This cannot be understood in terms of ordinary concepts, but nonetheless describes phenomena that are clearly observed and have been unambiguously confirmed. Both the created physical world and Jesus' basic nature defy ordinary understanding.

Jesus' position of leadership in the universe. A similar thought to that of Colossians 1:17-18 is found in Hebrews 1:3b, 4 and in the words by Paul as he comes to the end of the hymn of kenosis[6] in Philippians 2:9-11. The New Testament declares that at the present time the divine second person of the Trinity not only continues to uphold all of creation but has in addition been given leadership over all creation. The declaration of "Jesus is Lord" is just one way of expressing this.

Jesus' position in the redemption of the universe. Colossians 1:20, John 3:16 and Romans 8:19-23 declare that redemption is cosmic and is not just for humans. It extends to all of creation, with Christ Jesus as the agent of this cosmic redemption.

The biblical record points out that the incarnate Word, Jesus, has a scope and a mission that reach the entire cosmos, that he existed

---

[6]Here the Greek word *kenosis* refers to Jesus' voluntary, self-emptying of certain attributes and prerogatives while he lived here on earth.

before creation, that he is the agent of the Godhead who created the universe, that he upholds the universe in its consistent operation, that he is fully human and fully God, that he is the Lord of the universe, and that he is the agent of the redemption of the entire cosmos. The tendency to focus on only humanity, and thus think that Jesus simply died for people, is too limited and narrow. Instead, God through Jesus Christ has a cosmic outlook and a cosmic concern.

HEBREWS 1:1-4

The epistle to the Hebrews, classified as one of the general or catholic epistles, centers on Jesus as prophet, priest and king. The four verses under consideration here serve as an introduction to the doctrinal part of the epistle.

This passage functions as another of the great christological passages of the New Testament, and the attributes of Jesus Christ displayed here can be compared to those observed in the Colossians 1:15-20 passage. The passage affirms seven characteristics of the Son.

The eschatological character of the Son. The Son is the one through whom God has spoken in these "final days." The first verse states that in earlier times God spoke "many times and in many ways to our ancestors through the prophets." But in these "final days" God "has spoken to us through his Son" (Heb 1:2), and so there is a sense of finality and completeness in what Jesus said while here on earth among us.

The inheritance of the Son. "God promised everything to the Son as an inheritance" (Heb 1:2). Donald Guthrie points out[7] that, as we think of the created order, we need to be reminded that it belongs to Jesus Christ. This has some implications regarding our ecological responsibilities. The writer here wants us to understand that there was never a time when the Son was not the heir. The Son, also the creator, inherits what he has made. The writer to the Hebrews plunges us into deep thinking about the origin of the universe and the world,

---

[7]Donald Guthrie, *The Letter to the Hebrews*, Tyndale New Testament Commentaries (Leicester, U.K.: Inter-Varsity Press, 1983), pp. 64-65.

and the relationship and responsibility of humanity toward it.

The creatorship of the Son. The next phrase "and through the Son he created the universe" (Heb 1:2) is consistent[8] with what has already been observed in John 1 and in Colossians 1. God could have created the universe and all that is in it apart from the Son. But as the New Testament makes so clear, God chose the second person of the Trinity as the agent of creation. The sacred writers of John, Colossians and Hebrews were convinced, through the insight given by the Holy Spirit, that the One who lived among them was the One who created all.

The godliness of the Son. "The Son radiates God's own glory and expresses the very character of God" (Heb 1:3). The first phrase here expresses the same idea as in John 1:14, where eyewitnesses report, "and we have seen his [the Word's] glory, the glory of the Father's one and only Son." Guthrie writes that this means that the whole ministry of Jesus was evidence of God's glory.[9]

An important idea not expressed in other New Testament passages originates in the Greek word *hypostasis* (1:3), one of the richest words in the Greek language applied to Jesus, the Son. This word means "an exact representation of God's real being." The NRSV translates this word as "the exact imprint of God's very being," whereas the NASB renders it as "the exact representation of His nature." The translation used for this book (NLT) chooses "expresses the very character of God." All these reflect well the meaning of hypostasis. The Son is God, the Son is divine. And the thought here echoes Colossians 1:19, "For God in all his fullness was pleased to live in Christ."

The sustaining power of the Son. "And he [the Son] sustains everything by the mighty power of his command" (Heb 1:3). Just as in Colossians 1, the Son is declared to be responsible for the continuing stability of the universe, including the regularity of physical law and the constancy of the primary physical attributes of the universe. The implication of the sustaining power of the Son clashes with the deist im-

---

[8]Ibid.
[9]Ibid., p. 66.

age of God the clockmaker, who after creating the universe sits back and simply lets the cosmos develop and operate with no further involvement from God. Instead, the picture here of the Son is one who is continuously and actively involved in all aspects of the created order.

The cleansing power of the Son. The Son "cleansed us from our sins" (Heb 1:3). This phrase implies more than forgiveness, as cleansing is equivalent to making pure. Hence Hebrews 1:3 declares not only the upholding of the vast universe by the powerful word of the Son but also his intimate involvement with each of us in cleansing us of our sins.

The praise due the Son. In conclusion to this prelude to the epistle, the Son in Hebrews 1:3 is seen to have sat down (active, not passive verb[10]) at the right hand of God and in the place of high honor, for the Son merits recognition and a name far greater than that of the angels.

SUMMARY

Consistent with the entire New Testament witness, the second person of the Trinity is declared to be the agent by whom God created and actively upholds the universe. The New Testament clearly affirms the contribution of Christ Jesus to the understanding of creation in the Bible and adds to the Old Testament picture seen so far.

So that leaves us with the question, what about Genesis 1 and 2?

---

[10]George Gestakys (private communication).

Genesis 1:1–2:3
and Genesis 2:4-25

THE GENESIS 1 SIX-DAY CREATION account plays a prominent role in the creation-evolution conflict. The next chapter's discussion of the resolution of this conflict cannot take place in the absence of a careful and thorough study of creation in Genesis, to be done in the present chapter. Some surprises will follow.

There are misconceptions to dispel. The six-day Genesis 1:1–2:3 account is not the only creation material in Genesis. As noted in chapter two, Genesis 2:4-25 constitutes a second account, this being a one-day creation. In many instances the understanding of creation focuses only on Genesis 1 as *the* biblical account of creation. But to obtain a complete picture of the message of creation in Genesis, the existence of the Genesis 2 passage must be recognized and brought into the biblical creation picture.

It should already be clear to the reader that even the inclusion of Genesis 2 does not tell the entire biblical creation story, for the previous two chapters have focused on other biblical passages in both testaments in which creation plays an important role. The principle to be applied here is comparing Scripture with Scripture. This can be especially important when trying to ascertain the biblical outlook on complex and important issues that the Bible does not directly address and was not the first audience's concern. The contemporary creation-evolution issue falls under this classification.

SOME CONTENT AND CONTEXT QUESTIONS TO CONSIDER

In doing Bible study employing a method such as that presented in chapter three, important components include a careful consideration of both the content and the context of the passage of interest. The NLT translation of Genesis 1 and 2 (found in chapter one) constitutes a good tool for studying the textual content of these chapters. But before concentrating on content, the context of the passages will be considered. The following are among the questions to be considered in this chapter.

1. What is the literary structure and context of these creation passages?

2. What are the historical and social contexts?

3. Authorship—who and when?

4. How do these passages fit into the primeval prologue of Genesis (1–11)? into the entire book of Genesis? into the entire five books of the Pentateuch?

5. How do the two accounts compare? What is the significance of the comparison?

6. What was the intent of the sacred author (or editor of Genesis) in producing the two creation accounts? What role did they play in the life of the ancient people of Israel?

7. Why are these two accounts placed at the beginning of the Bible?

8. What is the genre of these passages?

Literary structure and context. The genre of both Genesis 1 and Genesis 2 is narrative, with a bit of poetry in both chapters. The type of narrative and the question of its literalness or nonliteralness will be considered in due course. Genesis 1 has an intricate literary structure involving the six days of creation. The content and structure of Genesis 1 carry significance, as the eight creation commands spoken by God (YHWH) are woven into the six days of creation in a beautiful and symmetrical pattern. The second three days (days four through six) parallel the first three days, with the first three days devoted to the formation of the heavens (the universe) followed by its filling in the second three days. This can also be expressed as the creation of spaces on the first three days followed by the creation of their inhabitants on days four through six. Gordon Wenham has suggested a structure for Genesis 1, which is found in table 2.[1]

Table 2. Gordon Wenham's Conception of the Structure of Genesis 1

Forming	*Filling*
Day 1 Light	Day 4 Luminaries
Day 2 Sky	Day 5 Birds and fish
Day 3 Land (plants)	Day 6 Animals and humanity

Wenham points out that the narrative has two poles, heaven and earth, starting in the heavens and moving to earth on days four through six, with the culmination of creation on day six when the spotlight falls on humanity (Gen 1:26-30). The structure can also be understood as "Days 1, 2, 4 *heaven* in contrast to Days 3, 5, 6 *earth*."[2] Genesis 1 emphasizes God as the careful planner, creator and evaluator of the creation events.

In contrast, the second creation account, in Genesis 2:4-25, consists of a simpler one-day account. One might be tempted to call it a story or a narrative, centered on humanity and God's intent and provision for humanity.

The two creation narratives fit into the overall literary structure of Genesis. The book of Genesis can be divided into two parts, the pri-

---

[1]Gordon J. Wenham, *Genesis 1–15*, Word Biblical Commentary (Waco, Tex.: Word, 1987), p. 7.
[2]Ibid.

meval narrative or primeval prologue, Genesis 1–11, and the patriarchal narrative, Genesis 12–50. As Wenham points out, the entire
book stands as a unity but is divided into sections, each section introduced by the Hebrew word transliterated as *toledot,* meaning "This is
the (family) history of." There are ten sections to the book in addition
to Genesis 1:1–2:3, which as a prologue to the entire book, stands
outside the remaining structure.[3] The outline of these sections is
given in table 3.

Table 3. Ten Sections of Genesis 1

	1:1–2:3	Prologue
1.	2:4–4:26	History of heaven and earth
2.	5:1–6:8	Family history of Adam
3.	6:9–9:29	Family history of Noah
4.	10:1–11:9	Family history of Noah's sons
5.	11:10-26	Family history of Shem
6.	11:27–25:11	Family history of Terah
7.	25:12-18	Family history of Ishmael
8.	25:19–35:29	Family history of Isaac
9.	36:1–37:1	Family history of Esau
10.	37:2–50:26	Family history of Jacob

Historical and social context and authorship. The ancient Israelite
culture, out of which Genesis grew, was primarily corporate in its
worldview. Existence in the community constituted an important
part of the life of the Israelites. When God set the process of redemp-
tive history into motion, he did not do this by addressing a single
individual or each individual; instead he chose to bring into being a
people through the promise to Abraham by means of his covenantal
promise of posterity, land and a divine-human relationship.[4]

Most of the ancient world was illiterate. As a result, the predomi-

---

[3]Ibid., p. xxii.
[4]David J. A. Clines, *The Theme of the Pentateuch,* Journal for the Study of the Old Testament Supplement 10 (Sheffield, U.K.: University of Sheffield, 1978), pp. 29-30.

nant way by which the Israelite community communicated was orally. When Genesis was put into its final written form, the primary quality that the inspiration the Holy Spirit gave to the ancient author was the ability to be faithful to that which he had received, most of which had been revealed earlier by God to the community and had subsequently been handed down from generation to generation by oral means. When this happened for Genesis and the rest of the Pentateuch is an open question. Gordon Wenham puts Genesis in its earliest form not before 1250 B.C., but not much later than 950 B.C.[5] Evidence exists indicating that perhaps the entire five biblical books of the Pentateuch were not in their final form until around the time of the Babylonian exile, with perhaps Ezra being the final compiler and editor.[6] The Pentateuch, a complex set of five books, is an anonymous work with no indication within the books of its authorship. Jesus refers to "the book of Moses" in his ministry as he and the early church connected Genesis and the rest of the Pentateuch with Moses. Certainly Moses was instrumental in the formation of important parts of the Pentateuch, but Moses died well before some of the events recorded there had taken place.[7] One possible way to view the Pentateuch, including the book of Genesis, is to say that it is Israel's look at who it was in light of its beginnings, and that the overall author is the community of Israel living out its life as the people of God within the land of promise and under God's covenant, with God-inspired representatives putting this faithfully into written form.

Genesis creation in context. The relationship of the primeval prologue to ancient Near Eastern writings. Throughout ancient times, people from around the world formulated their own accounts of how the cosmos and earthly life began. These creation stories offer the reader a glance at the cultural history and unity of humankind. Many

---

[5]Wenham, *Genesis*, pp. xlii-xlv.

[6]William Sanford LaSor, David Allan Hubbard and Frederic Wm. Bush, *Old Testament Survey: The Message, Form, and Background of the Old Testament* (Grand Rapids: Eerdmans, 1982), pp. 54-67.

[7]Tremper Longman III, *How to Read Genesis* (Downers Grove, Ill.: InterVarsity Press, 2005), pp. 45-46.

books have been produced that present collections of these creation stories. One such collection, *Sun Songs: Creation Myths from Around the World*,[8] contains stories of over fifty different people groups from North America, South America, northern Europe, central Asia, Mesopotamia, Greece, Africa, Egypt, the Far East, Oceania and the South Sea Islands.

A simple comparison of the primeval prologue, Genesis 1–11, with other ancient literature reveals that Genesis 1–11, including the two Genesis creation passages, parallels ancient Near Eastern traditions in many ways,[9] whereas the Genesis 12–50 patriarchal narratives and the remainder of the Pentateuch are uniquely Hebrew. Frederic Bush suggests that the voice of Israel speaks through the Pentateuch as a whole. The setting for Genesis 1–11 is the same as for the rest of the Pentateuch, namely, Israel herself and *not* the first generations of humanity in general.[10] And consequently, the Bible opens with a uniquely Israelite account of beginnings from their perspective.

However, ancient Israel as a nation was situated at a specific time and a specific geographical location. Ancient Israel was immersed in a repository of ideas and concepts about the beginnings of the world, the animal kingdom and humanity, for Israel itself was part of a larger ancient Canaanite-Semitic culture and society. These ideas and concepts of its neighbors it accepted, transformed, opposed or rejected, according to its own particular theology as revealed uniquely to it by God and as it reflected on its own history as a people.[11] The main structure of Genesis 1–11 parallels other ancient Near Eastern texts[12] that also contain stories of the creation of humanity, their development, their subsequent degeneration and the decision of the gods to

---

[8]Raymond Van Over, ed., *Sun Songs: Creation Myths from Around the World* (New York: New American Library, 1980).

[9]For example, see James B. Pritchard, ed., *The Ancient Near East,* vol. 1, *An Anthology of Texts and Pictures* (Princeton, N.J.: Princeton University Press, 1958).

[10]Frederic Wm. Bush, "The Historical Nature of the Primeval Tradition," in *Supplement to Old Testament Survey and Selected Readings,* pp. 23-34 (unpublished).

[11]LaSor, Hubbard and Bush, *Old Testament Survey,* pp. 68-75.

[12]Pritchard, *Ancient Near East,* vol. 1; Longman, *How to Read Genesis,* chap. 4.

send the flood, including a sacrifice upon leaving the ark. It is true that general similarities exist between the stories of Genesis 1 and Genesis 2–3 and the literature on origins of these ancient Canaanite-Semitic peoples. The same kind of relationship can be seen in Genesis 4, 5, 6:1-4 and the flood accounts of Genesis 6–9.

But it must be emphasized that this does not mean important, detailed similarities cannot be found between the biblical narrative and the Mesopotamian cosmology, particularly in the cases of Genesis 1 and Genesis 2 and 3. Both Genesis 1 and the other ancient Near Eastern literature present the same order of creation, and both conclude with the divine rest. Genesis 2 (and 3) are also recognized as derived from a background of Mesopotamian literature. Correspondence exists for individual events, symbols, conceptions and even technical terminology. Even though these similarities exist, *the overall teaching differs radically.* The biblical author draws from the same circle of topics in order to *speak against* the worldview presented in the other ancient Near Eastern literature.[13] For example, these pagan writings present a worldview steeped in polytheism. The Mesopotamian gods personify natural forces and know no moral principles. Humankind plays no special role as the highest created earthly being, made in God's image. Instead humans, the lowly servants of the divine overlord, relieve the gods of the drudgery of work and provide them with food and offerings. The biblical accounts proclaim the one true, holy God as the Creator, independent of the world. In the Mesopotamian accounts, creation results from conflict and struggle as the gods war against each other. In contrast, Genesis creation occurs in a harmonious way and results from God's careful plan as he simply speaks creation into being.[14]

Creation in Genesis stands beside the many creation accounts of ancient cultures worldwide, exhibiting striking similarities with those of ancient Israel's nearest neighbors. But biblical creation is sig-

---

[13]Ibid.

[14]Longman, *How to Read Genesis*, pp. 69-98; LaSor, Hubbard and Bush, *Old Testament Survey*, pp. 73-75.

nificantly different, as Genesis attributes creation and providence to
the one universal God, YHWH (or YHWH Elohim). And this makes
all the difference. As Christian believers and followers of Jesus, we rest
on this foundation of our faith.

   Genesis 1 and 2 in Genesis and the Pentateuch. As noted earlier, the
theme of the Pentateuch as a whole has been suggested by David
Clines[15] to be the partial fulfillment of the threefold promise by God
to the patriarchs: the promise of posterity, the promise of a divine-
human relationship and the promise of land. These promises encompass Genesis 12–50 and the other four books of the Pentateuch.
Clines points out that the promise to the patriarchs represents both
a divine initiative in a world where humanity has already fallen
deeper and deeper into sin (Gen 1–11) and also a reaffirmation of the
divine intention for humanity (Gen 1–2).

   The primeval narrative (Gen 1–11) does not constitute a complete
unit. This prologue, rather than being disconnected from the rest of
Genesis and the Pentateuch, functions as a true prologue to the patriarchal narratives of Genesis 12–50. The entire primeval narrative
moves with a single purpose, starting with the creation passage of
Genesis 1, then focusing on the first generations of humankind in
Genesis 2:4 through the end of chapter 4, with part of chapter 2 being
the second creation narrative. Then Genesis 5 marks the transition
from the antediluvian world to that of the flood, with the character of
the world being set forth in the conjunction of the nations in Genesis
10 and the Babel story in Genesis 11:1-9. Genesis 11:10-26 follows one
line of the family of Noah to Abraham (Gen 12), thus signaling the
transition to the patriarchal prologue. There is no major break between the primeval and patriarchal prologues, and hence the book of
Genesis should not be thought of as two independent units, Genesis
1–11 and 12–50, but instead as a whole. According to LaSor, Hubbard
and Bush, even though the call of God to Abraham is of crucial importance, it is simply one more step that God takes, begun early in

---

[15]Clines, *Theme of the Pentateuch*, pp. 29-43.

the primeval narrative, in his attempt to deal with the world that he has created and in which humans choose to sin.[16] David Clines agrees, when he writes that the theme of chapters 1–11 is, "No matter how drastic man's sin becomes, destroying what God has made good and bringing the world to the brink of uncreation, God's grace never fails to deliver man from the consequences of his sin."[17]

So Clines sees two threads in the first eleven chapters, first, the goodness of God, that the purposes of God for the world and for humanity are good, in contrast with the second, the sinful nature of humanity. He finds no break at the end of the Babel passage, but rather a unity to all of Genesis and the Pentateuch as a whole.[18]

Comparison of the two Genesis creation passages. Contextual questions having been discussed, the next step is to consider the content of the two Genesis creation passages.

One step in becoming aware of the content of these passages is to compare them. At first glance, it appears that even though there are a number of similarities, the two narratives differ in a number of ways, discussed below. First, we will examine the similarities.

Similarities. 1. God is the agent of creation. God is the active agent of creation in each narrative. God carefully plans, decides to create or to make, and then carries out his decision. In Genesis 1:1–2:3 a tight procedure consistently describes God's actions. First God says, "Let . . . ," then the creative act God has called for happens, and God pronounces the result good. It appears that God does not use any preexisting materials but speaks creation into being from nothing preexisting. Words such as *create* and *make* are used to describe God's actions. In the first three days of creation, the cosmic and terrestrial spaces (the environment) are created, and in the second three days these spaces are filled by what God creates.

The Genesis 2:4-25 passage is more of a flowing story or narrative. Once again God carefully plans, but this time with more attention

[16]LaSor, Hubbard and Bush, *Old Testament Survey*, pp. 75-86, 111-16.
[17]Clines, *Theme of the Pentateuch*, p. 76.
[18]Ibid., pp. 76-79.

given to humanity than in the cosmically oriented Genesis 1. Again God carries out his decisions, but this time his creative acts are described with words like *form* (from the dust of the ground), *plant, make, place,* and *make* (from the first person's rib). Here God consistently uses materials at hand to cause new entities to be formed or made. But it is God who initiates and carries out the creative process.

2. *Each account tells of the creation of life found on earth: animals, birds and a human pair.* At the end of each account all of these exist, but the order of appearance is somewhat different in the two passages.

3. *Responsibilities are given to humanity.* In each narrative certain tasks are assigned to humanity. Even though the tasks differ from passage to passage, the two sets complement each other. In Genesis 1:28 God directs the newly created male and female pair to (1) "be fruitful and multiply," (2) "fill the earth and govern it," and (3) "reign over the fish in the sea, the birds in the sky and all the animals that scurry along the ground." The Hebrew word translated in verse 28 as "reign" (over the fish) is the same word that in the previous verse is translated "govern." This word can also mean "have dominion" or "rule" and seems to clearly imply that humanity is to have leadership or governorship over the rest of creation. In terms of the first three directives to be fruitful, multiply and fill the earth, humanity is doing quite well in carrying these out. And these may represent the only commandments of God that humanity has truly fulfilled!

Genesis 2:15 fills out the instruction to govern in Genesis 1:28. Here God gives humanity direction in terms of the style of governorship (leadership) to apply over the earth and its inhabitants. God places the single person made from the dust of the ground in Genesis 2:7 into the garden to "tend" and "watch over" it. These Hebrew words are rich in meaning. The word translated as "tend" also means labor, work, cultivate and serve,[19] and the word translated as "watch over"

[19]Francis Brown, S. R. Driver and Charles A. Briggs, *Hebrew and English Lexicon of the Old Testament* (Oxford: Clarendon Press, 1951), pp. 712-14; William L. Holladay, *A Concise Hebrew and Aramaic Lexicon of the Old Testament* (Grand Rapids: Eerdmans,

signifies keep, have charge of, preserve, guard, be careful about, protect, save, revere, and be careful and attentive.[20] Hence the function of Genesis 2:15 is to clarify the type of leadership over creation declared by Genesis 1:28. Humanity's leadership is to be caring, nurturing, developing of creation's potential, along with a style that preserves and serves it.

Looking further, *tend* also implies that humankind is to develop the raw materials of the garden, allowing it to reach its inherent potential to produce what is good and beneficial, things that enhance all life on earth. This suggests that among the products derived from the garden's raw materials include good culture (art, music, literature), beneficial government to all, an economic system that enhances all people's lives, good family life, good technology, good science and a care for the earth, to name a few.

In a sense, the two directives of Genesis 2:15 serve as a check and balance. Yes, the raw resources of creation are to be developed and cultivated to produce those products that enrich all of creation. But in using these resources, whether they be the natural inanimate resources of the earth and the cosmos or the animate resources of all living beings, including humans, humanity is to do so in a nonexploitive and nonselfish way. Humanity is directed to care for the cosmos, the earth, living creatures and people. Humanity's leadership role includes watching and protecting. Humanity is to serve creation. Is it possible to lead and serve at the same time? Such a lifestyle is especially appropriate for those of us who affirm God and his creation and act as God's agents to help fulfill his intent for all creation.

The other task for the person of Genesis 2:7 is found in Genesis 2:19, to name the wild animals and the birds. Perhaps this implies that humanity is to investigate or study creation, as naming would imply understanding and classifying. Does this endorse scientific study?

4. Creation is God's intent. Each of the acts of creation results from the decision of God. God does what he sets out to do, and does it in

---

1971), pp. 261-62. To be referred to as BDB and H subsequently.
[20]BDB, pp. 1036-37; H, pp. 37-38.

an orderly way and as he intended. This is in stark contrast to the ancient Near Eastern creation myths in which creation comes about through conflict, the gods warring with each other and using humanity as slaves to carry out the drudgery of creation.[21]

5. *God's creation is very good.* The goodness of creation is explicitly declared or implicitly implied in each account. On five of the six creation days in Genesis 1, God declares that what he has made or created is good. After creation is completed on the sixth day, God looks over all he had made in Genesis 1:31 and sees that it is very good, is excellent.

Even though there is no explicit evaluation of creation in Genesis 2, by implication the tasks given the person in Genesis 2:15 are those that would aid in the good development of the creation and cause it to thrive. In addition, God provides for the single human of Genesis 2:7 a second person as an appropriate companion. God recognized that the single person is in some way incomplete, for God declares that it is not good for that person to be alone. It is clear in Genesis 2:25 that the person is full of joy after God has formed the second human.

Differences. 1. *Context in relationship to surrounding biblical passages.* One difference is that Genesis 1:1–2:3 is a "stand alone" creation narrative, a prelude to the rest of the primeval prologue and only addresses the topic of creation. On the other hand, Genesis 2:4-25 is part of a larger narrative of the first generations of humanity, Genesis 2:4–4:26, focusing on the creation of humankind, the Fall and the account of the first offspring, Cain and Abel.

2. *Timelines.* In Genesis 1 creation occurs over six days, whereas in Genesis 2 the entire creation takes place on one day. The NLT is not very explicit about this point, for the opening verse of the second narrative reads, "This is the account of the creation of the heavens and the earth. When the LORD God made the earth and the heavens . . ." (Gen 2:4). The Hebrew word translated here in Genesis 2:4 as "when" is the same word consistently translated as "day" in Genesis 1.

---

[21]Pritchard, *Ancient Near East,* vol. 1; Longman, *How to Read Genesis,* pp. 69-98.

Many biblical translations depict this word as "in the day," with "day" always in the singular. In any event, the creation events in Genesis 2 occur continuously, with no indication of a day coming to an end and a new day beginning. Regardless of the translation of that Hebrew word, in Genesis 1 there are six of them whereas there is only one in Genesis 2.

3. *Order of events.* The order of creation differs in the two accounts. The first two humans, male and female, are the final creation event in Genesis 1. This follows after the creation of plants, trees, animals and birds. But in the Genesis 2 narrative God forms a single human from the dust of the ground early in the sequence of events and before the creation of plants, trees, birds, animals and the second human. The sacred writer of Genesis must have deliberately altered the order of creation events in the two narratives. Why?

4. *The name and plurality of God.* In the first narrative God's name is consistently given as Elohim (God), whereas in the second narrative God's name is always YHWH Elohim (LORD God), sometimes written in English as Yahweh Elohim. In the first narrative both the singular and the plural are used in association with God, notably in Genesis 1:26-28, whereas in Genesis 2 LORD God is always singular. The use of both singular and plural in reference to God in Genesis 1 has been a source of puzzlement and discussion among theologians for two thousand years and has consistently given these theologians material for their scholarly papers and books.

5. *God's action in creation.* Three Hebrew words (transliterated *bara, asa* and *yasar*) are found in Genesis 1 and 2, denoting God's creative activity.[22] *Bara* appears only in the first narrative in Genesis 1:1, 21, 27 and 2:4. Its basic meaning is "to create," and it is used exclusively in the Old Testament to denote divine creation and what only God can do. *Bara* implies the initiation of an object and the absolute newness of what is created. This word is used in reference to

---

[22]BDB, pp. 427-28, 793-95; H, pp. 141, 284-85; R. Laird Harris, Gleason L. Archer and Bruce Waltke, eds., *Theological Wordbook of the Old Testament* (Chicago: Moody Press, 1980), pp. 127, 396, 701.

the creation of the heavens and earth (Gen 1:1 and 2:4) and three times to that of humanity (Gen 1:27).

Asa (Gen 1:25, 26, 31; 2:4, 18) means "to do" or "to make," and sometimes "to make a thing out of something else or into something." The word *asa* is much broader in scope than *bara* and implies primarily the fashioning of an object.

The third word, *yasar,* appears only in the second creation narrative, in Genesis 2:7, 8 and 19. Its meaning is "to form, shape or fashion" and implies a divine activity like that of a potter. In Genesis 2:7 God forms the human from the dust of the ground. In Genesis 2:19 God forms the animals and birds, also from the ground and as a potter. This word denotes various types of craftsmanship. In contrast to *bara,* the sacred author explicitly mentions the materials out of which God created as he used *yasar* to describe the creative act.

A comparison of creation of humanity in the two accounts deserves attention. In Genesis 1:27 humanity is made *(bara)* in the image of God, whereas in Genesis 2:7 the first human is made *(yasar)* from the dust of the ground, and later the woman is made from an already-existing rib of this first human.

6. *Motivation for the creation (formation) events and the first humans.* Genesis 1:26 reads, "Then God said, 'Let us make human beings in our image, to be like ourselves.'" Genesis 1:26 indicates that the decision of creating the first human pair on the sixth day involved more than one, in a council of the Godhead possibly. Three plurals, referring to God, are found in verse 26 in the decision to create these humans. But the decision to carry out this act of creation arises completely in Genesis 1:27 within Elohim (singular), as if Elohim is carrying out a detailed plan formulated in advance.

But in Genesis 2 it is always YHWH Elohim (the LORD God) who decides by himself and then carries out the decision to form or make. Many of the creative acts in Genesis 2 are in response to a situation that arises and are then performed by the LORD God. In Genesis 2:5 there are no people to cultivate the ground, and so in verse 7 God responds by forming a human, and among other things, God tells the human to tend and watch over the garden in verse 15. God finds the human to be alone and realizes this is not good (verse 18) and so forms the wild animals and the birds from the ground. But these provide no helper just right for him (verse 20). As a result God makes a woman from one of his ribs (verse 21) and brings her to him (verse 22). Then the man exclaims, "At last!" (verse 23). In contrast to Genesis 1, many of the creative acts in Genesis 2 arise out of a need related to the current state of the creation as observed by God, and so God responds.

Comments on the two accounts—significance of their existence, their differences and their placement in the Bible—intent of the Genesis author. There are two Genesis creation accounts. We have noted that the accounts differ in a number of ways. And they were placed at the beginning of the Bible, constituting the first two chapters of the Bible. Because we strongly affirm the Bible as our infallible rule of faith and hence take it seriously, these three facts call for some reflection. It would be simpler if there were just one account, Genesis 1 or Genesis 2. But since there are two accounts, it would be simpler if they agreed with respect to their common facts. Our thought is that each of these three notable characteristics represents the carefully formulated intent of the sacred writer (or editor). Can we ascertain that intent?

A possibility is that each of the two creation accounts represents different aspects of creation. Taken together, the two accounts form a more complete portrait of creation than either alone, with each contributing unique aspects. As discussed earlier, Genesis 1 presents an overall cosmic picture, with the focus shifting to the earth and humanity on the latter days of creation. Genesis 2 concentrates on humanity, specifically God's intent that humans be in relationship with other humans and his command that humanity develop and care for creation. Neither in itself completely covers all aspects of creation, and each plays an important role in its understanding.

Many people regard Genesis 1 as a literal account of the creation events, having contemporary scientific and historical relevance. This understanding seems unlikely to be correct. The state of affairs in biological science and in the study of cosmological and earth development differ in significant ways from the Genesis 1 narrative. This contemporary scientific work is likely closer to the truth than not.

Could there have been a purpose in the writing of Genesis 1 that goes beyond literalism? A purpose for which literalism is inappropriate? The sacred writer faithfully recorded both the scientific and the theological understandings of his ancient Hebrew community. These people were nomads whose scientific knowledge resulted from naked-eye observations of their surroundings on earth during both the day and the night. This probably was not much different from the scientific approach of their neighbors. The scientific and historical elements of Genesis 1 are a record of this knowledge. These people had no sophistication in terms of their scientific study. But God revealed himself uniquely to the Hebrew people, and their understanding of God resulted in religious convictions also expressed in Genesis 1. Although the general form of these stories in Genesis are the same as those of their neighbors, the theological outlooks differ significantly. Genesis creation served as the vehicle by which the ancient Hebrews responded to the creation stories of these neighbors. Underlying the cosmological surface in Genesis 1 is the metaphysical or theological understanding of the ancient Hebrews, and this set them apart from their neighbors. And hence their account of beginnings, even though in terms of an ancient cosmology, was cast with a theological understanding of the true and universal God, the God that we worship as Christians. We suggest that Genesis 1 in its most important role functions as a theological statement of the ancient Hebrews.

Genesis 2, using facts that differ from Genesis 1, tells a story of humanity's role in the creative order and God's intention for humanity. Genesis 2 ends with the joyous creating and uniting of the first male and female couple, completing the story of God's provision for humanity and humanity's assignment. How different our world would have been had humanity not started the spiral into degrading sin depicted in Genesis 3, involving the first couple and in Genesis 4 with the first family. God's intentions for humanity in Genesis 2 were wonderful, and he has not released the human race from the assignments given in Genesis 2 and Genesis 1. The sacred author uses a completely different approach from that of Genesis 1 in presenting the message of Genesis 2. The provision for a suitable companion is most effectively told through the depiction of just one human being initially created, God's desire to provide an appropriate companion equal to that person, God's attempting to provide this through the person's naming of the animals, and finally and successfully God's creation of a second person. It is clear that this last step was the answer.

Genesis 1 and 2 address different aspects of creation. But in presenting these, the sacred author casts his message, inspired by the Holy Spirit, in two accounts that contain significantly different facts. It follows that the biblical writer, in addressing his ancient hearers, chose a nonliteral genre by which to express one or both accounts. Our conclusion is that his purpose in doing so is the same as Christian writers' use of nonliteral genres. The important and complex theological truths being presented to the ancient Hebrews are most effectively cast in terms of the familiar—in this case in terms of creation concepts that were well known throughout the ancient Semitic Near East. Here is a case of God accommodating himself to the world of his chosen people, the ancient Hebrews. God chose not to give these ancient people the theological facts of creation one by one in a systematic and literal form, with any science contained therein conforming to our contemporary standards. Is there any hope they could have understood such a presentation? Instead God chose to formulate these deep theological truths in terms familiar to the ancients.

Why are the two accounts placed first in Genesis and hence first in the Bible? There must be an important reason for this. Because both deal with beginnings, the opening of the Bible would be a natural place for relevant aspects of creation. But a more important reason could be because of their significance. Recall the observation made in the previous two chapters: that biblical creation consistently addresses the most important topics. So it is quite possible that Genesis 1 and 2 are found opening Genesis and the Bible because they deal with important issues. Earlier it was noted that the entire structure of Genesis appears to have been well planned. It follows that the placement of these two chapters also reflects careful planning by the biblical author (editor), consistent with their importance.

The genre of the Genesis creation accounts. The differences noted between the two Genesis creation passages leave us facing an issue, how to account for the differences among the facts. Is it best (is it faithful) to understand these passages in a literal way, in particular the Genesis 1 creation narrative, as so many people have done and continue to do? Asking the question in another way, do we find historical and scientific information in Genesis 1 (and 2) with which we can compare current historical and scientific understandings of beginnings? The differences make it difficult to argue that both passages are literal, for the facts are too different between them. But some would object that regarding the Bible as containing nonliteral material moves us toward heresy.

Why would any sacred biblical author consider writing a passage in a nonliteral way? Recall the earlier discussion of the use of a nonliteral genre, such as story, by respected Christian writers. They have found that in certain cases such a genre is the best choice by which to most effectively convey important theological concepts. Their idea is to use a nonfactual or nonliteral vehicle to most effectively carry out their theological goals and to present truth.

Imagine for a moment that you the reader are the sacred author of Genesis, and you want to put into writing your fellow ancient Hebrews' unique understanding, revealed to the community by God, of all aspects of beginnings as found in Genesis 1 and 2. And remember that since the Bible is incarnational, an appropriate form of the writing may refer to that with which the ancient Hebrews were acquainted or had experienced in some way. A scientific treatise meeting contemporary standards would be meaningless to the ancient Hebrews. Furthermore, the author would need to receive dictation from God and would have no idea about what he was writing. This does not seem to make sense.

We are given a number of hints within the passages that Genesis 1 and 2 each function in a nonliteral way. They include

- the different and conflicting factual content of the narratives
- the existence of two narratives
- the conflict between the historical and scientific content and contemporary understanding

This last point needs some discussion. Many Christians do not like the conclusion of cosmologists and earth scientists that the cosmos and the earth are billions of years old, for they see a conflict with the creation in Genesis 1 in six days. Even more Christians do not like the contemporary Darwinian evolutionary status in biology. The criteria for evaluating this scientific work is not, "I can't see that (fill in the blank) is possible," or "The conclusions of (fill in the blank— cosmology, earth science, biology) don't make sense to me." The criterion for evaluating any scientific proposal or idea is, is there evidence supporting this? Can this idea be used to predict other scientific phenomena correctly? We have seen that much of scientific understanding goes well beyond our common sense, for the phenomena of beginnings involve enormous time spans and/or distances that play no direct role in our ordinary lives. And yet these phenomena are part of God's creation, and this part of creation has only been open to careful investigation in the last one hundred or two hundred years, millennia since the completion of the Bible. The contemporary status of cosmology, earth science and biology is understood and accepted by the overwhelming majority of professional scientists working in these fields, whether they are Christians or not. It provides the starting point for any research by professional scientists. Hence, for a well-meaning but nonscientific Christian to simply dismiss these scientific results in the absence of scientific justification should be carefully questioned. If scientific results seem to conflict with a given reading of the Bible, careful consideration should be given to the possibility that a somewhat different way of understanding the Bible might be more appropriate.

Our conclusion is that most likely the Genesis creation narratives are not to be read literally but rather are to be read as stories that have two levels of truth. First, the Genesis 1 account represents the ancient Hebrews' understanding of cosmic history and development, including the earth and its inhabitants. But the sacred author was not as concerned about the factual details as he was about clearly presenting theological concepts understandable by his intended audience, the ancient Hebrews. Genesis 2 has a different theological purpose, and the author did not hesitate to tell a story that contained this truth. The theological messages in these chapters represent the second level, the story under the story of both creation accounts. The first level is irrelevant today because of scientific and cosmological historical understanding. But the second level, the theological level, inspired by the Holy Spirit, contains the message that is relevant for all people yesterday, today and into the future. And it is at this level that the importance of Genesis creation comes to the forefront. In short, we propose that Genesis 1 and 2 are nonliteral accounts, housed in an ancient cosmology and a story of humankind's beginnings, whose purposes are to teach important theological truths.

If we are on the right track, the next step is to determine the theological concepts that the Genesis 1 and 2 author was proclaiming to his hearers and to us.

Summary

The purpose of this chapter is to take a careful look at the two Genesis creation passages. Among the relevant features of these passages are three that are particularly pertinent to our discussion.

1. The ancient people of Israel, like almost every culture worldwide and nearby in the Semitic ancient Near East, produced creation stories that reflected who it was as a people as it resided near other Semitic peoples. Israel's location influenced the structure of the Genesis creation accounts and other features of the primeval pro-

logue (Gen 1–11). Israel's identity as a people is reflected by the transformation of the content of the pagan stories into what is found in Genesis. This content reflects their relationship with and understanding of the one true God, the true Creator of the universe, the God and Father of our Lord Jesus Christ.

2. The two creation narratives that open our Bible differ in a number of significant ways, leading to the conclusion that the accounts are not to be read literally. One consequence of these differences is that the two accounts together give a more complete picture of creation than either alone, Genesis 1 having an overall cosmic concern and Genesis 2 focusing on humanity. But the differences negate the possibility of reading both literally. Eliminating literalness leads to regarding these passages as narratives (stories) whose purpose is to teach theological truth.

3. God has a high regard for creation and a concern that creation thrive. Humanity is given the task of governing, developing and caring for creation in a watchful, nurturing and serving way.

7

Genesis 1 and 2
as a Worldview Statement of
the Ancient People of Israel

CREATION IN THE BIBLE—SUMMARY AND SIGNIFICANCE

In the previous three chapters, all important biblical creation passages have been studied, with the motivation of applying the principle of comparing Scripture with Scripture to this topic. The goal has been to come to a better understanding of Genesis 1 and 2 than is possible in the absence of knowledge of these creation passages. Doing so aids in the determination of applications of these passages to twenty-first-century issues.

Creation in the Old Testament, especially as portrayed in Isaiah 40 and Job 38–41, deals with difficult, complex and significant issues facing the people of Israel and an individual; it deals with exile and the suffering of an innocent person. Creation also plays an important role in worship in the temple and the synagogue. Many of these Old Testament passages reiterate aspects of Genesis 1 and 2, resulting in a consistency about the theology of creation throughout the Old Testament.

Creation references are much more limited in the New Testament. One important emphasis is to identify the agent of the Godhead who is responsible for both creation and upholding the universe from day to day: the Word, the Son, Christ Jesus. The topic, the future redemption of all of nature (including humans), is addressed in Romans 8. There is no hint of any scientific description of nature as the purpose for any of these passages. The sacred authors had other important things in mind. Our next task is to finish the consideration of Genesis 1 and 2 and to complete the justification of the thesis of the book, namely, the purpose of the creation accounts in Genesis as declaring the worldview of the ancient people of Israel.

GENESIS 1 AND 2—SCIENTIFIC CONSIDERATIONS

It was pointed out in the previous chapter that although the two Genesis accounts have similarities, they differ in a number of ways. On the surface these portray two different ancient accounts of the Hebrews' scientific and historical understandings of creation. These do indeed depict events in the history of the universe and our earth that actually took place during its development. The universe and the earth have come into being along with the stars, sun and moon. Life arose on earth, including but not limited to vegetation, fruit-bearing trees, animals, fish and bird life, and humans. The union of male and female occurred. And these events have taken place in a definite historical order. These Genesis accounts depict real history and real science. No problem yet. But do these accounts depict history and science that meet today's standards? In other words, are the creation accounts of Genesis up to the caliber we would expect of contemporary scientific investigations or historical research? Whether the answer is yes or no, problems arise and result in the long-standing creation-evolution conflict.

Looking at this question from the contemporary scientific point of view, it has been pointed out that the sciences of cosmology, physics, geophysics and biology together have formed a picture of the development of the universe and the earth with all of its features. This scientific work leads to the conclusion that the universe is 13.7 billion years old and the earth 4.5 billion years old. Scientists have traced the development of the raw materials of the universe—such as the fundamental particles, nuclei and atoms, along with life from the first self-replicating molecules—to life as we observe it today. An open question remains, how were the first self-replicating molecules formed? Work remains to be done on this and a number of questions. But scientists are confident that the overall picture will not change significantly even as new discoveries are made.

Science is an agnostic enterprise. Topics such as God or spiritual matters are not the concern of science, so these are not part of scientific thinking or scientific research. It is similar, for instance, in reading a book on the operation and features of Microsoft Office or trying to understand techniques in processing digital photographs by studying (puzzling over) the *Adobe Photoshop Elements* book. One does not expect to find discussions of spiritual matters or references to prayer, the holy Trinity or the gifts of the Spirit in such books. In doing word processing or enhancing photos, discussions about God are not only completely irrelevant but also inappropriate. (However, one might need to pray for an understanding of the technical information in these books.) The absence of addressing matters of theological interest does not imply that these are promoting atheism; instead, we expect to find a narrow focus on the subjects at hand, namely, writing on a computer and digital photography. However, if these authors go beyond the topics of the books, let's say in making comments about God or any other religious matter, we would rightly criticize that, saying to the authors, "Stick to the subject." But this is not to say that the information contained in these publications is useless for Christian purposes. The author of a book intended to be of use to Christians might very well refer to the Microsoft Office book to find useful information in preparing a manuscript on prayer, or a Christian photographer could find the Adobe book helpful in producing stunning nature photographs for a book that calls for praising God. And so, even though these technical books are completely agnostic in terms of any contents about Christianity or God, they can be legitimately useful for Christians in their service to God.

So it is with science. Science is an empirical and limited enterprise that is theistically agnostic, concerned only with the *how* mechanisms of nature as pointed out in chapter two. It is *methodologically* naturalistic; however, it is not *metaphysically* naturalistic. And the difference between methodological naturalism and metaphysical naturalism is immense. Science is metaphysically neutral. But even though science does not address theistic issues (and rightly so), it does provide information of interest to Christians in terms of beginnings, as follows:

- The universe and the earth are old—billions of years, and certainly not thousands of years.

- The universe and all therein have developed slowly and continuously over time from a simple beginning. This includes the life of the earth and of humanity.

The book of nature (science) and the book of Scripture cannot in principle contradict each other, for they both proceed from the same Author. Conflict between scientific and theological understandings of beginnings should not exist. Is it possible that science could aid in understanding the Bible, in particular Genesis 1 and 2? Scientific results could be used to put fences around possible interpretations of passages of Scripture such as Genesis 1 and 2. This will be considered shortly. In the meantime, some strictly theological thought about Genesis follows.

GENESIS 1 AND 2—THEOLOGICAL CONSIDERATIONS AND WORLDVIEW
A summary of important conclusions.
1. Genesis 1 and 2 are incompatible when considered from the literal point of view. There are simply too many differences between the two passages. A logical conclusion is that these passages should not be read literally.

2. A literal reading of Genesis 1 results in a number of conflicts with a broad range of modern science—cosmology, physics, geophysics and biology. If the literal reading of creation in Genesis is valid,

then these modern scientific fields are significantly in error in their results and probably in their methods. This scientific deficiency would imply that science beyond the sixteenth or seventeenth century up to now is wrong. Is this really possible or even probable? We think not.

The question raised previously is, is it possible that the science and history contained in Genesis constitute a story on the surface, but that the message below the surface is something far more important? When considering all the factors leading to this point, an affirmative answer appears to be consistent with this understanding. This does seem to us to be a satisfactory conclusion. The genre of the surface level of each Genesis creation account is story, related to observations and experiences of the ancient Hebrews. But there is a second level, a story beneath the story, composed of narrative that teaches the theology of the ancient Hebrews. Of the two levels, the most important is the story beneath the story. The upper-level stories are vehicles for the theological teaching. Part of the thesis of this book is that the purpose of the two Genesis creation passages is best understood as proclaiming theological truth, but this truth is *not* in blow-by-blow historical or scientific accounts of creation (in the contemporary sense of historical or scientific enterprises). Instead, these are creation accounts that work together below the surface to articulate something *much more important* and, because of this importance, were placed at the beginning of our Bible.

Derek Kidner[1] understands Genesis 1–11 as describing two opposite progressive themes, first, God's orderly and good creation, with its climax in the creation of human beings as responsible and blessed, but second, the folly of Babel. The theme of the spread of sin throughout Genesis 3–11 is only the negative aspect of the overall theme of these chapters. The pattern according to which creation proceeds in Genesis 1 and 2 is the positive aspect of the sin/judgment/grace motif of chapters 3–11. In Genesis 1 and 2 there is obedience followed by

---

[1]Derek Kidner, *Genesis: An Introduction and Commentary*, Tyndale Old Testament Commentaries (Downers Grove, Ill.: InterVarsity Press, 1967), pp. 13-14.

blessing. The narrative as a whole moves toward blessing in Genesis 1, first on the living creatures, then on humanity and, finally, on the seventh day (Gen 2:3). The theme of Genesis 2 is also blessing, moving toward God's intention for humanity to be in mutual relationship. This is the positive counterpart to the main theme of the primeval history, and as such affirms from the beginning to the end that all from God is very good.

James Sanders[2] suggests that in the lengthy process of canonization, the Bible (and the Pentateuch) emerged, humanly speaking, out of the experiences of ancient Israel, as this community asked questions of their authoritative traditions in terms of worldview questions. Sanders maintains that the proper function of the text continues to be in dialogue with the heirs of the community as they continue to seek answers to these primary worldview questions. And it follows that, as distant heirs of that community, these narratives play the same type of role for us today.

Worldview. We have come to the point where we can suggest that Genesis 1 and 2 together constitute a worldview statement of the ancient Hebrew people, and because of the importance of this statement, these accounts are found at the beginning of the Bible. Worldview is generally associated with a general outlook on life and the world, and consists of the most basic assumptions about what is real and good. A worldview expresses the general orientation of everything a person thinks and does.[3] A worldview statement addresses a number of vitally important questions, questions whose answers for an individual set forth how that person is to live or for a group of people define their basic philosophy. Genesis 1 and 2, in the story beneath the story, work in a complementary fashion in together presenting a coherent worldview of ancient Israel, and this is the primary reason for their being both a part of the Bible and the

[2]James Sanders, "Hermeneutics," in *Interpreter's Dictionary of the Bible*, supplementary volume, ed. Keith Crim, Victor Paul Furnish, Lloyd Richard Bailey Sr. and Emory Stevens Bucke (Nashville: Abingdon Press, 1976), pp. 402-7.
[3]Dallas Willard, *Knowing Christ Today* (New York: HarperOne, 2009), pp. 39-44.

opening narratives of the Bible. Worldview questions and brief answers given by the ancient people of Israel in Genesis 1 and 2 include the following:

How is it that things exist? Genesis 1 and 2 together make the clear assertion that the universe, including our earth with all its inhabitants, is the result of the planning and ability of the God that the people of Israel affirm and worship. It is God who carefully plans and speaks creation into being, and it is God who forms living creatures including humanity. All of this is the result of God and not because of Marduk or any of the deities of Israel's neighbors. Creation accounts by these neighboring peoples stand in significant contrast with the Israelite understanding of the One who is responsible for creation.

The question of faith or identity—who are we? This question has been addressed earlier. Humanity is the product of a specific decision of the Godhead. ("Then God said, 'Let us make human beings in our image, to be like ourselves'" [Gen 1:26].) Humanity is the climax of God's creative work in Genesis 1, and God places humanity at the highest place in creation. This is the understanding of the ancient Hebrews of humanity's position from a cosmic perspective. Genesis 2 has more of a focus, not on cosmic matters, but on humanity and its task of the development and care for creation.

Who are we? Between Genesis 1 and 2 we find that humanity is the result of God's specific plan and his ability to create. Humanity has been given the highest place in creation and is its leader, developer and caretaker. Humans are also to be in mutual relationship with other humans. And if one reads further in Genesis 3, one finds that humans are intended to be in relationship with their Creator. All of this results from God's intentional plan in creation.

What does God think of us and the rest of that which exists? God has a very high view of all of creation. At the end of each creative day, God almost invariably declares that what he has created is good. When the creation had been completed on the sixth day, "then God looked over all he had made, and he saw that it was very good!" (Gen 1:31).

In Genesis 2 it is clear that God has a high regard for humanity, as he provides "a helper who is just right for him" (Gen 2:18). God's high view of humanity and all of creation is also seen in his assignment for humanity to govern, develop and care for creation.

The question of obedience or lifestyle—what are we to do? A detailed discussion has been given earlier, and the reader should be referred to that discussion. In summary, Genesis 1 indicates that humanity is to govern, to have leadership over creation. The style of leadership is clearly specified in Genesis 2:15 to be one that develops the raw materials of creation to make all sorts of beneficial things for the enhancement of life, from good art to good economics. This developmental activity is to be one that serves, cares for and preserves creation. And we are to be in relationship with one another.

Together Genesis 1 and 2 address and answer the four worldview questions for the ancient Hebrews in a unique way and in significant contrast to the viewpoints of their pagan ancient Near Eastern neighbors. Genesis 1 and 2 emerged out of the experience of ancient Israel, as this community listened to God and considered these primary worldview questions.

Hence, the focus, especially of the first narrative in Genesis, is not on the scientific aspects of creation, but rather on topics of significantly more importance than science. To primarily concentrate on scientific aspects, ancient or contemporary, *completely* misses the point that the ancient biblical author intended. In concentrating more on humanity, Genesis 2 fills out the creation account of Genesis 1 in such a way that, working together, the two creation narratives present the ancient Hebrew worldview.

This worldview understanding brings the creation-evolution conflict to an end, for now Genesis 1 does not refer to current science. Hence, there is no conflict between Genesis 1 and current scientific thought. It is completely consistent for a person to be a serious scientist, even a biologist, earth scientist or cosmologist and, at the same time be a serious follower of Jesus, using the entire Bible as that person's foundational book and guide to life. And, just as God declared the entire creation to be very good (Gen 1:31), so a scientist can praise

God for every scientific discovery. For each scientific discovery makes it clearer and clearer just *how* God creates, but not *why* he created. Genesis 1 and 2 do tell us that God is the creator and *why* he created, but Genesis 1 and 2 do not give us any information about *how* God created. The mechanisms, or the *how,* of creation are the purview of the scientific community.

CONSEQUENCES OF UNDERSTANDING GENESIS CREATION AS WORLDVIEW
There are gains and there are losses as a consequence of regarding the creation narratives of Genesis 1 and 2 as the worldview statement of the ancient Hebrews.

Gains.
1. *There is now rapprochement between science and Christian faith.* If Genesis 1 addresses worldview concerns only, that is, theological concerns only, then no one need be concerned about the scientific statements of Genesis 1 being contrary to those of contemporary science. No longer do Genesis 1 and science need to be in accord. The Genesis 1 references to the formation of the universe, the earth and life are only intended, through nonliteral story, to support the point that the sacred writer was making in addressing worldview questions. The cosmological and earthly aspects of all that exists are mentioned only as entities that were planned and created by God, and there is no intent to describe the mechanisms of creation from a scientific point of view that would have any relation to a current scientific account. As a result, the creation-evolution conflict disappears, and the only significant criticism that Christians might have with contemporary science is when atheistic scientists stray beyond their science and make unjustified remarks about Christianity or religion in general, or if they maintain that the only worthwhile knowledge is scientific knowledge. In addition, the application of scientific knowledge to nonscientific topics must be examined closely in order to determine the validity of such an application, and when appropriate, Christians rightly should point this out. Finally, it is important to

realize that the worldview understanding removes any negative evaluations that science might claim relative to Christianity, in particular, Christian support of an outmoded scientific outlook.

One might ask the question, well, what about evolutionary biology? The worldview interpretation of Genesis 1 and 2 implies that there is nothing in contemporary Darwinism that threatens Christianity and Christian doctrine, as long as Darwinism is confined solely to science. Applications of Darwinism, such as to social engineering, have no validity. On the positive side, DNA research shows that humans have a close relationship to all living things and that all living things share a common ancestor. These are results of important scientific studies, yet they merely provide information limited to the *mechanisms* of aspects of creation and have no relation to the theological understanding of the creation of humanity. As long as it is realized that there is no information of current scientific interest in Genesis 1 and 2, and as long as it is realized that there is no theological information in any current scientific study, then no conflict between science and Christian faith should arise in relation to these creation accounts. End of controversy—finally.

2. Doors will be opened wider for presenting the gospel to our educated friends. It is no longer necessary to attack the current status of cosmology and earth science over the age of the universe and the earth. It is no longer necessary to attack the current status of evolutionary biology. If we no longer insist to our unbelieving friends that Genesis 1 and 2 give accurate, contemporary scientific information, then possibly insurmountable barriers to presenting the gospel to these friends are removed.

Most people with even a rudimentary knowledge of current science are aware of the scientific thought of a universe and an earth billions of years old and of the success of evolutionary biological science. For people who are not yet Christian believers, the requirement that they buy into the idea of a young earth or young universe, along with anti-Darwinism, as part of the Christian belief system puts up significant and invalid barriers for these unbelievers. The opening of the door to belief is unnecessarily too narrow. These "scientific" barriers make Christianity seem like a nonsense religion, a religion that is hopelessly out of touch, which requires its followers to turn off their eyes, ears and brains when stepping into church. But this barrier to evangelism need not exist.

3. *Doors will be opened wider to welcoming theological ideas in influencing the direction of scientific inquiry.* If scientists, even nonbelieving scientists, can come to understand that Christianity no longer sees science as an enemy, there is the possibility that some scientists will understand that science and religion could work together on issues of mutual interest. There is already some movement in this direction. For example, scientific investigations on the effect of prayer on the healing process are being carried out. As the relationship between science and Christian faith continues to warm, we expect that there will be increasing interplay and investigative projects in which science and Christian theology participate as partners, each contributing to the investigation and understanding of questions of mutual interest.

4. *A biblical hermeneutic that is well suited to faithful Bible reading and that is applicable to complex contemporary questions will have shown itself to be helpful.* Christians are rightly urged to read the Bible and to draw important lessons from it. But how many readers of this book have been given instruction on *how* to read our Bible? As has been pointed out, the principles of Bible reading are pretty simple and straightforward, but Bible reading does require a systematic approach in working with content and context, with the goal of the reader getting the writer's point. The application of the Bible to contemporary questions that are not a part of the biblical world can be a complex and difficult process, one that requires the greatest of skill in gleaning from the Scriptures an answer to a contemporary question. In such cases, the most careful and thorough approach to biblical teaching relative to the particular question can minimize possible misunderstanding.

5. *Scientific progress in biology, geology and cosmology can now be celebrated as encouraging signs of God's wisdom, power, care and faith-*

fulness in his creation. Each piece of scientific progress can now be regarded as further answering the question of *how* God created, and each answer should evoke praise from believing scientists and from Christians in general. As Howard Van Till points out,[4] the ability for the universe, including our earth and its life, to develop over time in a way that science can understand in terms of empirically observed data is a sign of the careful planning of God in creation. Here is evidence that God endowed the universe with the potential to develop under his laws, as observed by scientists, in the way that it has. This is not evidence that leads to an atheistic understanding of the universe but rather is confirmation of Romans 1, forming the starting point of a natural theology. As Job learned, our world is wonderful and mysterious but sometimes paradoxical, and the more we learn of it, the more reason we have to praise God who creates and sustains through the Son.

If the worldview viewpoint is accepted by the Christian community, then all Christians will be able to joyfully and thankfully receive news of scientific progress and will have more and more evidence of the wonder and magnificence of God's creation. Adoption of the worldview understanding will bring significant gains to Christianity.

Losses.

1. Literalism as the only faithful way to read the Bible will no longer apply in some cases. The incarnational character of the Bible shows it to be both a thoroughly divine book but also a human book. God in his wisdom used human authors, their humanness, and the cultural and historic context by which to give his word to humanity. It has been pointed out how this fully divine and fully human understanding is clearly seen in the incarnation of Jesus.

Identification of genre will result in abandoning the reading of some biblical passages literally, passages that might on the surface

---

[4]Howard Van Till, "Partnership: Science & Christian Theology as Partners in Theorizing," in *Science and Christianity: Four Views*, ed. Richard F. Carlson (Downers Grove, Ill.: InterVarsity Press, 2000), pp. 214-20.

appear to support such a reading. The case of Genesis 1 and 2 falls under that category. *2. In certain cases simplicity is lost in trying to find biblical answers when approaching contemporary issues.* In some cases thorough work is required in using the Bible to investigate questions that the Bible does not directly address. Prooftexting is inadequate in these cases and may lead to error in the attempt to gain a valid biblical perspective. Instead, a systematic interpretive method must be applied.

Taking a worldview outlook from Genesis 1 and 2 clearly results in gains that far outweigh the losses.

Subject Index